BRAZILIAN
Jiu-Jitsu
A TRAINING MANUAL

BRAZILIAN

Jiu-Jitsu

A TRAINING MANUAL

Ricardo Da Silva and Edward Semple

THE CROWOOD PRESS

First published in 2006 by
The Crowood Press Ltd
Ramsbury, Marlborough
Wiltshire SN8 2HR

www.crowood.com

British Library Cataloguing-in-Publication Data
A catalogue record for this book is available from the British Library.

ISBN   1 86126 759 2
EAN   978 1 86126 759 7

Disclaimer
Please note that the authors and the publisher of this book do not accept any
responsibility whatsoever for any error or omission, nor any loss, injury,
damage, adverse outcome or liability suffered as a result of the information
contained in this book, or reliance upon it. Since martial arts can be dangerous
and could involve physical activities that are too strenuous for some individuals
to engage in safely, it is essential that a doctor be consulted before undertaking
martial arts training.

Photography by Mike Holdsworth

Designed and typeset by Focus Publishing, 11a St Botolph s Road, Sevenoaks,
Kent TN13 3AJ

Printed and bound in Singapore by Craft Print International Ltd

Contents

Dedication

This book is dedicated to Harry Knowles, John Moore and Keith Wilson. Thank you for all your help and guidance, but, most of all, for your friendship.

Acknowledgements

The authors extend their sincere thanks to Tim Radcliffe, Rodrigo Silva, Ralf Langen and Mike Holdsworth. Tim and Rodrigo feature in the pictures in the book and have worked exceptionally hard to ensure that the technical detail is both accurate and precise. Ralf proof-read the book and was brutally honest with his opinions throughout. Bob was its editor and, without his incredible patience and support, it would never have been published. Mike took the pictures and brought real life and colour to the techniques described. Mike has twelve years experience of specializing in martial arts photography and the unique experience of having photographed a wide range of martial arts in several martial arts schools, dojos and academies. He provides the photography for a number of teams, individuals, clubs, equipment suppliers and action actors/screenfighters. Mike is based at Shepperton Studios where he supplies promotional photographs for films and television. Finally, Ricardo would like to thank Keiko who have provided him with the sponsorship that he has needed to develop as a fighter and an instructor. It is Keiko equipment that is worn for the photographs shown here.

Foreword

I was introduced to Brazilian jiu-jitsu several years ago as a very blinkered international judo player. I was to quickly discover that this amazing sport is, in my estimation, the ultimate martial art. Within one session a new world had opened up before me and, quite honestly, I felt humbled by my great void of knowledge of ground work. This came as quite a shock to me. After some twenty years at the top of my sport judo I believed that I had a good command of most ground work techniques and could predict most attack scenarios.

I soon came to the conclusion that by combining the new skills I was learning in jiu-jitsu I could become a more accomplished judo player since the two complement each other in many respects. Now that the pressures of international competition have been lifted from me, I now find myself in the enviable position of practising both these sports for the pure enjoyment of doing so. Sleeping Storm gives me the environment to do just that and the coaching standard is top class.

I can wholly recommend jiu-jitsu to up-and-coming judo players as a means to expand their range of techniques, and the fact that this sport has a lower physical impact on the body makes it accessible to the older player as well. Ed Semple at Sleeping Storm allows you to explore both sports and this book will give any enthusiast a fascinating insight into the origins of Brazilian jiu-jitsu and a comprehensive tour of the range of techniques employed. Whatever your grade and age I am confident that the rewards are there for the taking, if you are prepared to open your eyes!

David Southby
5th Dan and Former Commonwealth and International Judo Champion

1 The History and Development of Brazilian Jiu-Jitsu

The Birth of Ju-Jitsu

No one can definitely say where ju-jitsu began but India is the most likely place. But what is beyond dispute is that the Japanese were responsible for refining it into a very sophisticated grappling martial art. Ju-jitsu was developed in Japan during the feudal period and it was an art devised for warfare, designed to be vicious, practical and effective, incorporating striking, weapon disarmament, take-downs, throws, chokes, locks and pins. With the abolition of the feudal system in Japan, modifications had to be made so that the art of ju-jitsu was more suitable for practice in a more peaceful time. Ju-jitsu was no longer needed for the battlefield, instead, its practice was to change so that the art became relevant to a population which lived predominately in peace. This more modern approach was to place more emphasis upon the grappling techniques of the old art and develop the locks, take-downs, chokes and strangles.

Jigoro Kano

In the late 1800s Kano developed his own system of fighting from ju-jitsu and named it judo. He began receiving ju-jitsu instruction in the 1870s, but by this time it was out of favour and considered as the outmoded, violent legacy of the past. Because of this, Kano sought to modify ju-jitsu and bring this beautiful art back into the mainstream as a valued piece of

Japan s heritage. To achieve this, Kano felt that it was critical that he did not simply teach his students how to fight but also gave them a sense of social responsibility. So he banned all students from fighting for money or in challenge matches and instead instigated the first formalized competitions. Although the techniques he was teaching were essentially those of ju-jitsu, he called his unique interpretation of ju-jitsu judo because he wanted to distance himself from the old, very violent style of ju-jitsu and place much greater emphasis upon his students personal improvement and responsibility rather than just their fighting skills. Judo was designed so that the practice of this art was relatively safe but still continued to be realistic and effective. Kano felt that the major weakness of ju-jitsu was in the old training methods still used in the schools of his time; he believed in the techniques but not in the old methods of teaching. Ju-jitsu had too many techniques that would simply maim or kill and their practice obviously made it impossible to use this art as a hobby or a sport. Yet, without practice under combat conditions, how would a student know that he had the ability to apply all the techniques learned in a real life situation?

Kano s answer to this, and his real genius, was to take the techniques that he wanted from the old ju-jitsu schools that allowed students to fight in practice and competition but not to kill nor maim each other. He wanted to teach techniques that could be continually practised in a combat setting and under the stress of attack yet allowed students to live a normal, everyday life. To teach fighting skills for the normal man rather than fighting skills for the soldier or professional fighter was his aim. The major contribution judo made to the practice of ju-jitsu was the concept of rondori. Rondori is simply sparring, fighting under sporting rules, and the rules that govern judo were developed so that two students could fight without the specific techniques that could result in death or permanent disability. These rules allowed students to practise frequently with less injury and lead a normal life. Judo took ju-jitsu from the battlefield and put it into the modern dojo, and thereby allowed people to study a martial art as a hobby, a sport and a form of self-defence. However, judo still retained the effectiveness of a proper fighting art. After a contest between the older styles of ju-jitsu and judo at the Tokyo police headquarters judo was named the national martial art of Japan and was the official art used in law enforcement in the late 1800s.

Judo is simply a style of ju-jitsu and not a separate martial art; the ju-jitsu schools Kano studied at all contributed to the development of judo and the techniques that it is based upon. It is almost ironic that by removing so many deadly techniques from ju-jitsu Kano actually created a more combat-effective martial art for the modern practitioner. Kano studied the jikishin-ryu style of ju-jitsu where students were not only expected to master fighting techniques but also to develop into generous and responsible individuals. A fundamental aim of judo was to emphasize the moral and social development of a student as well as his fighting skills. From kito-ryu ju-jitsu, Kano developed one of the fundamental principles of judo — the breaking of an opponent s balance, the key to successfully applying any throwing technique in judo today. However, it was from the fusen ryu style of ju-jitsu that judo was to take and develop most of the ground fighting techniques that would become such a central part of judo and Brazilian jiu-jitsu.

In 1900 Kano s judo students challenged the fusen ryu ju-jitsu school to a contest. Such a contest against a classical ju-jitsu school was common and a contest that the judo fighters of that time usually won. However, Kano s students were about to fight a ju-jitsu school dedicated to the art of ground fighting and at this time judo had virtually no ground fighting techniques. Kano s students won their contests predominately with throwing techniques and the fusen ryu fighters realized that they could not compete with the throwing techniques of their opponents but that they could compete if they took the fight to the ground. Rather than win by ippon (throwing your opponent flat on his back), they would win by submission on the ground. So the fusen ryu ju-jitsu students looked to their superior ground fighting skills to dominate and beat their judo opponents. The fusen ryu students went straight to the guard position, lying on their backs with their legs wrapped around their opponents, in order to control their opponents and then apply their submission techniques to win their fights. This guard position is still a principle position in Brazilian jiu-jitsu and one that we shall cover in detail later. Kano realized then that if judo was going to be a complete fighting art then it needed to have a full range of ground fighting techniques to match the effective throwing techniques he had developed in the stand-up position. So, with instructors from other ju-jitsu schools and the fusen ryu school of ju-jitsu, he developed the ground fighting techniques that would define judo and ultimately Brazilian jiu-jitsu.

Maeda — the Messenger

In 1897 Mitsuyo Maeda started his judo training in Japan, he had a wonderful talent for it and quickly established himself as one of the most promising young students in the Kodokan Dojo, the dojo Kano had established to teach and promote judo. In 1904, at the age of 26 and already with a 4th Dan black belt, Maeda was offered the opportunity to go to the USA with one of his instructors Tsunejiro Tomita. The object of the visit was to put on a judo demonstration at the West Point Military Academy. The visit was not a great success, the Americans did not understand the techniques nor really understand what Tomita and Maeda were trying to teach them. In frustration, one of the students challenged Maeda to a fight. The student was a wrestling champion and thought that he had won the fight because he had pinned Maeda to the floor. However, Maeda had no understanding of Western wrestling and continued to fight until he got his opponent in a joint lock and made him submit. The students then wanted to see Tomita fight because he was the teacher and they all assumed that he must be the better fighter. However, Tomita had come only to demonstrate and not to fight; he was in his forties and past his prime but, to save face, he felt that he had no choice but to fight. Unfortunately, his opponent was a much larger American who was able to pin him to the floor easily under his greater weight so that Tomita could not

move and was forced to give up. The experience was a humbling one for Tomita and Maeda and it was here that the latter first started to develop his style of fighting for the smaller man. The Americans tended to be much bigger than the Japanese and Maeda needed to develop a style of fighting that allowed a smaller man not just to beat but to dominate a much bigger, more aggressive opponent.

Tomita and Maeda parted ways with the former going to the West Coast and the latter staying in New York. Maeda wanted to set himself up as a teacher and establish his own dojo in the USA but the Americans did not take well to his Japanese style of teaching and none of the students stayed long enough to develop as fighters. To make money, Maeda accepted fights against anyone who wanted to take him on and it was in these contests against much bigger men from several different fighting backgrounds that he was to refine his judo skills into such an effective fighting system. Maeda travelled all over North, Central and South America as well as Europe, fighting in professional contests and using his superb judo skills to dominate and beat his opponents. At 1.65m (5ft 5in) and 69.7kg (154lb) he was relatively small and yet he fought anyone willing to take them on, even if they were much larger and heavier than he. He was to have over 2,000 fights and, incredibly, was to remain undefeated.

In 1915 Maeda left America and settled in Brazil which was to become his home although he continued to travel abroad for fights and tournaments. Maeda loved Brazil, where he felt that he was accepted much more for who he was and that the USA was a much more racist environment for a Japanese to live in. What is more, his fame as a fighter allowed him to do something in Brazil that he had never been able to do in the USA — it allowed him to set up and open his own successful dojo. The Brazilian people loved him and people from all over came to train at his dojo. It was when a local politician Gastao Gracie asked Maeda to teach his son Carlos that the magic really began and a dynasty created.

The Gracie Family and a True Dynasty

To begin with, judo and jiu-jitsu were seen as similar and Kano struggled to show the difference between the two and to popularize his art. To most people, judo was merely a collection of the strongest techniques from a number of different jiu-jitsu styles. So, if judo was such an influence on Brazilian jiu-jitsu and judo and jiu-jitsu were so similar, why is Brazilian jiu-jitsu not simply called Brazilian judo? Although Maeda was a judo student he came from a background that was particularly strong on ground fighting techniques and much of what he brought to judo would have come from the fusen ryu ju-jitsu school. Judo is an art that puts a particular emphasis on the sporting side of fighting and the development of students both morally and socially. Maeda had no interest in this side of the sport, he was a prize fighter, he fought for money and he judged and developed his fighting skills purely on the criterion of whether he won fights. Maeda refined the judo skills he had learnt so he that would win fights against opponents of all styles, sizes and abilities. Being relatively small, he knew that it was on the floor that he would dominate and win. Judo evolved from the need to create a fighting system that could be practised in peaceful times in a relatively safe environment, but in contrast Brazilian jiu-jitsu went back to the street

and was developed from the need to create a fighting system that would dominate and defeat other fighting styles and systems in the contest arena. It was this different approach to judo that Maeda bought to Brazil with him and passed on to the Gracie family and that has defined the evolution and development of Brazilian jiu-jitsu ever since.

His travels before settling in Brazil also played a great part in his theories of effective combat techniques and how to train. He had beaten all comers in challenge matches, from boxers to wrestlers, street brawlers to prize fighters (even challenging Jack Johnson, the heavy weight boxing champion of the time who declined), so, in terms of technique, he was moving away from judo. When fighting he would use anything that would work, this was due to both his ju-jitsu background before training in judo and his huge experience of no-holds-barred challenge matches. He even insisted in calling his art ju-jitsu rather than judo, possibly because his need to fight in such a way was not allowed under the strict rules and doctrine of judo.

Carlos Gracie was the third-generation descendent of an immigrant from Scotland. He was born in 1901 to Gast o Gracie, a Brazilian politician. Carlos was the smallest of five very competitive brothers, the others being Osvaldo, Gast o, Jorge and Helio. Carlos became a student of Maeda when he was 19, but Maeda was getting old by this time and Carlos took only a year of lessons from the great man. Eventually Carlos taught his brothers the moves Maeda had taught him and so the family tradition of Gracie jiu-jitsu was born. Carlos and his brothers made a name for his family by fighting in demonstrations and street fights, taking Maeda s unique approach and developing it into their own brilliant and unique form of jiu-jitsu. Later on Carlos would use other Brazilian instructors and fighters to keep constantly refining and developing his fighting techniques to create the Gracie jiu-jitsu fighting art. Carlos Gracie opened his first training school in 1925 and from this point on the Gracie fighting art of Brazilian jiu-jitsu never looked back. What made Maeda s style of ju-jitsu, and ultimately the Gracie style of Brazilian jiu-jitsu, so effective was the constant exposure of these men to the fighting arena. What defined both Maeda and the Gracie family, and therefore their skill as fighters, was their willingness to fight anyone from any background. They believed absolutely in their skill and technique and thus they had the confidence and skill to take on and defeat anyone and everyone. Gracie jiu-jitsu schools throughout their history have issued a challenge to fighters from all styles and schools to come and fight them without rules. It is in these no-rules fights, or what were to become known as vale tudo (Portugese for anything goes) fights, that the Gracie family and their students would evaluate, refine and develop the techniques. The family had little time for stylized patterns of practice or complex technical movements that helped a student to gain a higher belt or grade, they had one interest and one only — the development and execution of techniques that would defeat their opponents as quickly and efficiently as possible in the arena.

Carlos Gracie was a similar fighter to Maeda because, like him, he was relatively small at 61kg (135lb) and, also like him, would fight anybody, regardless of size, weight or fighting style. Carlos was never defeated and became a legend in Brazil. His tradition of open challenge to anyone and everyone is still a fundamental part of Brazilian jiu-jitsu. His most famous contests were against a Japanese fighter called Giomori. Carlos drew with his much larger opponent twice, once by the sporting jiu-jitsu rules and the second time in no-holds-barred vale tudo. Carlos Gracie died in 1994 at the age of 92 and, like Maeda, his brilliance, skill and confidence inspired a new generation of fighters. However, he was not the only notable fighter in his family, his brothers also did much of the fighting and played a central role in developing Gracie jiu-jitsu. Helio was, in fact, the most successful fighter and, in his long and illustrious career, lost only twice. Helio was a courageous fighter who, in true Gracie style, won against fighters from all kinds of the martial arts, including boxing, judo, wrestling and kick boxing.

Most of his contests were no-rules fights and many of these were brutal affairs against much bigger and stronger men, but in what is considered the longest jiu-jitsu match in history, Helio Gracie fought a former student Santana. He was a student of the Gracie family for twelve years and fought more than twenty times for the Gracie Academy. However, Santana and Helio had a falling out and decided to settle their differences by fighting each other vale tudo. According to Rorion Gracie (Helio s son), Santana had betrayed Helio, his teacher, and criticized him publicly in a newspaper. They fought in 1957 to a packed stadium with the whole country watching on television or listening on radio, such was the huge interest in the fight. It was an epic encounter, lasting well over 3hr, an old photograph shows Helio driving his elbow into Santana s face from the guard position. But Santana was an intelligent, tactical fighter and played the waiting game until Helio, the older man, began to tire, when Santana launched his own vicious and violent counterattack. Santana, in true Brazilian jiu-jitsu style, slowly ground Helio into the floor; he used the head butt to good effect, forcing Helio s eyes to swell and shut. He tried to counter by using vicious heel kicks to the kidneys to wear Santana down. Three hours and 45min into the fight the two separated, they were on their knees facing one another and gasping for air. Santana recovered and reacted first and kicked Helio in the head. He went down from the blow and the fight was finally over, this was to be Helio s last fight. It was now down to the next generation of the family to take up the mantle and defend the family name. Carlos s son Carlson now entered the arena at the young age of 17; he took immediate revenge for his family and viciously defeated Santana in their first meeting. Carlson was to go on and fight Santana another six times, he won four and drew two. Carlson was also relatively small at 72.4kg (160lb), but he is acknowledged as one of the best Gracie fighters ever and as having had a huge influence on the technical development of Gracie jiu-jitsu. He altered many of the techniques his uncles had taught him because of his small stature and relative weakness and was to refine and develop many of these techniques so that they became even less reliant on strength and conditioning. He is quoted as saying that he could not get out of certain of the positions that he had been taught by his uncles so he had to invent new techniques to help him to escape from them.

The judo Maeda first taught in Japan gradually disappeared but it flourished on the other side of the world in Brazil under the guidance of the Gracies. The fights that the Gracie school had with schools in Europe, the USA and Central and South America blossomed under the name of vale tudo. A Japanese martial arts journalist wrote, Perhaps one day Gracie jiu-jitsu will come home and compete in the fighting rings in Japan. It took a little longer than he had probably hoped for but this has come to pass as Rickson Gracie, Royler Gracie, Renzo Gracie, Jean Jacques Machado and other Brazilian jiu-jitsu fighters have fought in Japan and reignited the interest there for this style of fighting. The male descendents of the Gracie family are all taught the family fighting art and encouraged to represent the family in the Gracie Challenge , an on-going invitation to fighters to prove their fighting superiority. Two notable fighters are Helio s sons Royce and Rickson. The first helped to popularize Gracie jiu-jitsu in the USA, Japan and around the world through his successful fights in the Ultimate Fighting Championship. This is a no-rules contest in an octagonal cage ring and Royce entered the ring, like his father before him, to challenge fighters from different fighting styles such as boxing, wrestling, karate, muay Thai and kick boxing. Like his father, he usually fought much larger opponents and with great success. Rickson has now become the acknowledged current champion of the family and is considered by many to be the best Brazilian jiu-jitsu fighter alive today, as well as one of the top fighters in the world.

Schools and Disputes

Through the last fifty years many Brazilian jiu-jitsu schools have opened and broken away from the original members of the Gracie family, making subtle changes and differences to the art. Gracie jiu-jitsu, Machado jiu-jitsu and Brazilian jiu-jitsu are all different schools from the same art. Rio de Janeiro was the base for the Gracie family and between 1940 and 1960 the family opened four Brazilian jiu-jitsu schools there. For

Brazilian jiu-jitsu the Gracie schools were the most popular, but these schools were not the only judo and Brazilian jiu-jitsu schools in the country nor the only ones to be innovative and successful. Many other wonderful teachers and fighters contributed to the technical development and popular success of Brazilian jiu-jitsu. Brazil has attracted relatively large Japanese communities to cities such as S o P aulo and it is in these that both judo and Brazilian jiu-jitsu have thrived. So teachers of both have come to Brazil and left their mark on Brazilian jiu-jitsu. Mehdi, a judo master from France, arrived in 1949 and still teaches there, his students include the Brazilian jiu-jitsu black belts Mario Sperry, Rickson Gracie and Sylvio Behring. The influence of judo on Brazilian jiu-jitsu is immense and a fundamental part of whence it originates. The immense contribution that the Gracie family made to Brazilian jiu-jitsu was not to invent this style but to develop the old style of judo into a more effective rules-free style.

The first split in the Gracie family occurred in the late 1960s. In 1967 the first Brazilian Jiu-jitsu federation was created by Helio and a system of grades and belts was developed. He was keen to standardize and to organize the style of Gracie jiu-jitsu he had been so instrumental in developing into one that could be spread across Brazil. Clarity was his aim so that standards could remain high and undiluted. However, Carlson was developing his own team of fighters and his own style of Gracie jiu-jitsu and in many ways he felt that he had continued the technical development of Gracie jiu-jitsu. Inevitably there was tension between the two generations of the family, each feeling that its approach was the correct one. These two sides eventually fell out with the Helio Gracie school arguing that the Carlson

Gracie school promoted a way of fighting that relied too much on strength and not enough on technique. This kind of argument has come back again and again to divide different schools of Brazilian jiu-jitsu. Just as in feudal Japan, where there were different schools of ju-jitsu all putting their unique interpretations into practice, so there are different schools all over Brazil, all teaching the same techniques, but all putting their own interpretations and modifications into practice. As a result, Brazilian jiu-jitsu is an art that continues to grow and develop. No two schools will teach exactly the same techniques and each will keep refining the ones it teaches so that it has an edge in competition.

The splits within the Gracie family, and the differing directions that the factions took, have continued to multiply over the years. Carlson is considered the father of sports Brazilian jiu-jitsu and has worked hard to take it down the same path as judo and to get Brazilian jiu-jitsu recognized as an Olympic sport. However, it is the tradition of no-rules fighting and of fighting any opponent from other martial arts that has captured the imagination of the public and, most importantly, of American television. It was the Gracie family that bought The Ultimate Fighting Championship to America and the American television audiences that were dazzled by the skill and brilliance of the Gracie fighters. The Championship is a no-rules contest in an octagonal ring, where fighters from any art can compete. The Brazilian jiu-jitsu fighters were to dominate this arena defeating fighters from boxing, wrestling, karate, muay Thai, kick boxing and other sports. The USA was to see that Brazilian jiu-jitsu had been technically developed specifically for mixed martial arts competition. The octagonal ring was the ideal platform for Brazilian jiu-jitsu fighters to show just how devastatingly effective they are against those from other fighting arts. It was here in this ring that the world woke up to the Brazilian jiu-jitsu phenomenon. Now any mixed martial arts fighter knows that great stand-up skills are not enough on their own to make him an effective fighter in mixed martial arts. Any participant must always look to his strengths to dominate and win fights, but without good ground fighting skills a mixed martial arts fighter is going to have to struggle. Brazilian jiu-jitsu has raised the standard of mixed martial arts and made many fighters have had to re-evaluate the skills necessary to be a complete and effective fighter.

The Gracie family have been responsible for much of the modern development of Brazilian jiu-jitsu. The term Gracie jiu-jitsu was used to describe the difference between that first taught by Maeda and the family s improvement of the art through the twentieth century. However, now Gracie jiu-jitsu has spread all over Brazil, the USA and much of the world many more champions of this great art are not family members nor from Brazil. These champions are all contributing in their own way to the progress of Brazilian jiu-jitsu by constantly improving on techniques and developing new ones. Most of the basic movements may still come from Gracie jiu-jitsu but, as the art develops, the term Brazilian jiu-jitsu has become more common and many now feel that as it spreads outside the country one day Brazilian jiu-jitsu will eventually be called jiu-jitsu again. Brazilian jiu-jitsu has developed over the years and continues to do so today because it is influenced by all the other arts that its practitioners come up against. So many different martial arts have come to Brazil that Brazilian jiu-jitsu has been refined against many different styles. What we now today see in countries such as the USA as mixed martial arts and as a relatively recent development was common in Brazil over a century ago. The great fight described earlier between Santana and Helio is a good example of this. Santana has been described as a wrestler, judo player and Brazilian jiu-jitsu fighter. The truth is that he had probably trained in a mixture of all three and the fact that he was one of only two fighters ever to defeat Helio Gracie means that he was effective in both the stand-up position as well as on the floor. Brazilian jiu-jitsu continues to grow out of the mixed martial arts arena and this is why it has captured the imagination of fighters and the public alike.

What Lessons Can Brazilian Jiu-Jitsu Pass on to the World of Martial Arts?

The world of martial arts is divided into hundreds of different ones, each claiming to be better and different from one another. The politics of many of these can lead to a bewildering array of different associations and governing bodies for just one art. What is more, none of these bodies or associations will recognize one another and so they divide students of the same art. The idea of the Sleeping Storm Dojo when we first set it up was quite simply to look at what united the martial arts world and not what divided it. There are currently fifteen different martial arts taught at the Dojo and they all have something unique to teach us. No one art is better or worse than another and the Sleeping Storm Dojo is home to arts from all over the world — Japan, Brazil, China, Korea and many other countries. Sleeping Storm Dojo was set up in the belief that a dojo is simply a sacred place of learning and development. This wonderful mix of arts has benefited the students of each at the Dojo. Each student is much more aware of the skill and discipline that each art demands of its students and the different strategies, tactics and techniques that define it. A large part of Sleeping Storm Dojo s appeal as a place of learning and development is that students can compare and refine their techniques and skills with students and instructors of other arts. Each student can learn from the others and help all at the Dojo to continue to develop and improve.

Brazilian jiu-jitsu found a ready home at Sleeping Storm Dojo because its practitioners are not insular in their practice or outlook. The world of mixed martial arts has made Brazilian jiu-jitsu fighters focus and adapt to the strategies and techniques of other arts by necessity. A Brazilian jiu-jitsu fighter will probably have a much better understanding of the skills and strategies of a boxer than a judo fighter would. This is because most judo fighters only fight other judo fighters and so are not so well equipped to thrive in mixed martial arts. The comparison between Brazilian jiu-jitsu and judo is a useful one because both are products of the same place and time, but their evolution could not be more different. Today Brazilian jiu-jitsu fighters have a more sophisticated ground game, whereas judo places much more importance on standing techniques; judo is much more of a sport and therefore has many more restrictive rules; judo does not allow leg locks, neck cranks nor hands on the face. The rules have over the years put more and more emphasis in competition on throwing techniques so that judo players have become less and less effective on the ground. The sporting rules of judo mean that if a player is pinned by an opponent for 30sec he will lose the match. Brazilian jiu-jitsu has no such time restraints on the ground and so a Brazilian jiu-jitsu fighter is more patient on the floor because he has the time to develop a situation. A judo player can win a fight by just holding someone down, but a Brazilian jiu-jitsu fighter must develop a dominant position into a submission, thus Brazilian jiu-jitsu produces more accomplished and confident fighters on the floor. The inclusion of judo in the Olympics and the resulting move to make it more television-friendly has meant that changes in its rules have restricted this once great art and returned the focus once again to standing techniques. Brazilian jiu-jitsu, in contrast, is a progressive style of ju-jitsu, ever changing and developing. Once a technique is developed and used in competition other fighters will begin to design counters to that technique, making it a constantly changing and evolving art. The formality of judo has taken it to the Olympics and made it a very popular sport. However, this formality, the restrictive rules and the move to emphasis stand-up techniques at the expense of ground work techniques has diluted its effectiveness in the mixed martial arts. Instead, Brazilian jiu-jitsu has developed into an art that defines effective ground fighting and, as a result, is an essential part of mixed martial arts competition. As long as there is an interest in mixed martial arts, and dojos such as Sleeping Storm where different arts can be practised under one roof, Brazilian jiu-jitsu will thrive. The lesson that it has passed on to the world of martial arts is simply that we all have something to learn from one another, and that will make us better, more skilful and more effective.

2 Important Training Drills

To study a martial art successfully it is vital that the student can produce the movements he learns smoothly and quickly. Any form of jiu-jitsu will always be based upon the simple principle that your opponent is bigger, stronger and more aggressive than you. The Brazilian jiu-jitsu fighter, as any such fighter would, will always look to technique and skill to defeat his opponent rather than brute force and aggression. This may sound obvious in theory but, in practice, the Brazilian jiu-jitsu fighter must be confident, smooth and quick, but, above all, be relaxed in the use of any technique he tries to apply. The principle of technique overcoming brute strength does rely on precision of movement. There is no secret to becoming a good Brazilian jiu-jitsu fighter, all it requires is practice, practice and yet more practice. With this comes confidence, smoothness and speed of movement, this is the platform upon which good technique is developed and maintained. It is usual in a Brazilian jiu-jitsu class to use the warm up to learn and reinforce the important movements needed to practise this art. Fifteen martial arts have found a home at Sleeping Storm Dojo and, as the owner of the Dojo, I have always been struck by the intensity and application with which Brazilian jiu-jitsu instructors teach and train. Nothing is wasted and every moment of the class is utilized, and both the warm up and the cool down are used to work on basic skills and movement. As a result, these periods are a longer and more significant part of a Brazilian jiu-jitsu class than of most other martial art classes. Most Brazilian jiu-jitsu classes will run for 2 or $2^1{}_2$hr, and part of the reason for this is that the warm-up and the cool-down will usually run for at least 30min each.

The drills and exercises that are described in this chapter all work on the important movements that you will need to develop as a Brazilian jiu-jitsu fighter and would be common to any Brazilian jiu-jitsu class that you might attend. These movements are a basic part of your warm up, and educate your muscles to perform some of the most fundamental movements. The movements practised in these drills are used in many of the different escapes, many of the transitions between positions and many of the submissions common to Brazilian jiu-jitsu. The principle of doing these drills in every training session is simple, to make it easier to memorize them and to make them smooth and reflexive. Many of these drills will help you to understand the principles of certain moves. All the sweeps you will learn have the same objectives, which are to break your opponents balance and to use his momentum to obtain a dominant position while you maintain a solid base and good balance throughout the movement. The sit-up drill described here will help you to develop many of the essential skills necessary to acquire good sweeping techniques. If you take the time to really learn these drills you will find it much easier to understand and learn many of the techniques and moves described later. You should get to know each drill well; do not worry if these are difficult at first, take your time and learn them all properly. They cover all the basic moves that you will use from white belt right up to black belt. When you

Forward roll.

Pass the arm under.

begin to fight you must remember that your body and mind should be well prepared. Any fight is unpredictable and opportunities to finish one are few and far between against a skilled opponent. This means that it is essential that you have the know-how to do all the moves and drills that you learn on both sides. Of course, depending on whether you are left- or right-handed, certain techniques or drills will always be easier for you to perform on one side than on the other. Always improve your weaknesses through training and make sure that you can perform all the moves and drills on both sides with the same speed and smoothness of movement.

Front Rolling Break-fall

This technique is a fundamental skill in any grappling martial art. If you attend any judo or Brazilian jiu-jitsu class you will see this move practised over and over again. This is because the primary aim of judo or Brazilian jiu-jitsu is to throw your opponent to the floor. I believe that this move is so important that every martial arts practitioner should learn this technique. However good you are at fighting in the stand-up position there is always

Break your fall.

the chance that you may be thrown or knocked to the floor. It is absolutely essential that you can fall safely. If you can do so, prevent injury and remain aware of what is going on around you, then you are still in the fight and able to defend yourself. If you fall awkwardly it is likely that you will be injured and unable to defend yourself before the fight has really started. Remember, the Brazilian jiu-jitsu fighter wants to get to the floor as quickly as possible because it is there that he is going to cause his opponent the most problems. Quite often a fighter is happy to take the throw from his opponent

19

Backward roll.

Sit back.

mat that you are on the floor since not everyone on the mat will necessarily be able to see you at any given time. On a harder surface it is not recommended that the left arm slaps the floor since this may cause injury and it is unnecessary if you are not on a matted surface training.

Always practise on both sides because you will not be able to choose which side an opponent will throw you on to. Sometimes, when I am watching a class, the students will do the drills only on their better side, which will hinder their progress later. As you are learning, try to do the technique correctly and become equally comfortable at performing it on either side.

Backward Rolling Break-fall

This technique is also a fundamental skill for any grappling martial art, because if you can be thrown forwards you can also be thrown backwards. Again, just like the first drill, if you attend any judo or Brazilian jiu-jitsu class you will see this move practised repeatedly. The primary aim of it is simply to fall safely and to prevent injury while remaining aware of what is going on around you so that you

because he is confident that, once the fight is on the floor, he will have the skills to finish the fight. If you do not have the correct technique to fall properly you will get hurt, so a good Brazilian jiu-jitsu fighter must be able to go to the floor without injury.

The Technique
Start by taking a step forward with your right leg, then bend your back and tuck your head in between your legs as you put your right arm between your legs. Now, roll over your right shoulder. The body should roll and then end up on the left side, with the impact dissipated along the entire length of the body. Do not cross your legs. Notice that the left arm hits the mat to reduce the impact and, more importantly, to make a noise. This noise alerts others on the

Roll over one shoulder.

Finish on your knees.

are still in the fight. As has already been mentioned, the Brazilian jiu-jitsu fighter wants to get to the floor as quickly as possible, and so a good fighter must be able to do so without injury and with confidence. This move is very common and useful when you are actually fighting and so it is essential that it becomes second nature through your training.

The Technique

From standing, bend the legs as if to sit down on a chair, but continue down to sit on to your buttocks. As you bend down, push your arms out in front of you. This prevents you from putting your hands down instead of your buttocks and potentially breaking your wrists. As you touch the floor, roll on to your back and over one shoulder, so that you end up with your knees back on the mat. As you sit down on your buttocks and roll, backslap the mat. Again, this important as we have seen and prevents someone from stepping back on to you. As with the first technique, this not recommended on a harder surface since it may cause injury and it is unnecessary if you are not on a matted surface training.

Hip Escape Drill

This is a crucial move that you need to learn as so much of Brazilian jiu-jitsu is about flowing from one position to another while moving your opponent s body where you want it to go. The use of the legs and the hips is vital to so many of the moves and techniques practised in Brazilian jiu-jitsu and this move is at the core of most of the sweeps, escapes and transitions used. A position that all fighters will try to obtain is the mounted position, and this is one of the first you will learn here. The mounted position is a dominant one from which you should have excellent control of your opponent s body. From it you will be able to attack your opponent with a huge

21

Hip escape drill.

Turn your body on to the left side.

Push your hips out to the right.

Repeat on the other side.

variety of attacks. If your opponent is mounted on you, you must try and escape from this position as quickly as possible because you are very vulnerable. This drill will help you to learn the escape and to put your opponent in a less dominant position and a more favourable one for yourself. If you cannot do the proper hip escape and hip escape drill you will struggle as a Brazilian jiu-jitsu fighter.

The Technique

Lie on your back with the right knee raised, turn your body to the left and slide your hips to the right side so that you end with your right leg straight and your left knee raised. Use both hands to push downwards on your left side, parallel with your left leg. This is the same move for the escape from the mounted position (as if someone were sitting on your chest) and in a fight you would use your hands to push your opponent s knee away. Your finishing position should be the same as the initial one, but with the left knee raised and your body turned to the right. From this position you must do the move again from the other side. In this way you will gradually move down the mat, moving your hips from right to left and left to right. The movement will in time become second nature and provide the basic skills you need to move on the floor when fighting.

Hip Escape Variation

This drill is specifically designed to train a fighter s ability to move his hips. So much of Brazilian jiu-jitsu relies on your ability to use your legs and hips. It is with your legs, and therefore with the most powerful muscles in the body, that you will tend to control your opponent s movements. Even if your opponent is on top and pinning your arms or head down, a Brazilian jiu-

Hip escape variation.

Push your hips to the right.

23

Pass the left leg under.

Body facing forward.

Finish on your knees.

jitsu fighter can use his legs and hips to escape and create attacking opportunities. A fighter s use of the hips is crucial in preventing an opponent from controlling the fight when he is on top. By moving your hips and turning on your side you can move, unbalance your opponent and create the opportunities you need to win the fight from underneath. Once you have mastered the hip escape this move can be developed and used as a very effective counter to an opponent who is trying to get around your legs and attack you from the side. The attack from the side when you are on the floor is one greatly favoured by Brazilian jiu-jitsu fighters because this is an area of potential weakness in your opponent. It is important that you can counter such attacks and this drill will help you to develop the bodily movement you need to rely on when countering such an attack.

The Technique
Lie down with your knees bent, push your body up the mat by using your left leg and move your hips to the same side. As you move your hips to the side, pass your right leg underneath your body. You will finish lying on your front. This can be a vulnerable position to end in if you do not keep hold of your opponent. It is normal when you finish in this position that you keep hold of your opponent s leg so that you can then push him to the floor by putting your shoulder on his hip. By breaking his balance in this way you can quickly turn defence into attack and reverse the position you were originally in. If you do not get hold of his leg your opponent will go straight to your back. Be careful and remember, with this drill, that in a fight you must keep hold of your opponent s leg. And again you must make sure that you can do this drill comfortably on both sides of your body.

Neck Drill

The neck drill is the first one that is not about improving technique but about improving conditioning and fitness. If you regularly practise Brazilian jiu-jitsu in a class or at a club you will have to spar. This part of the class is seen as essential in developing your skills and an ability to flow from one technique to another. It is quite normal that half the class is given over to sparring. This is a physically demanding martial art that will require you to maintain a good level of physical conditioning. There are two chapters at the end of the book diet and fitness training for Brazilian jiu-jitsu; these are recommended reading as they will help you to get into shape. This drill concentrates on strengthening the neck. Many of the techniques that you will learn will be attacks to the neck since Brazilian Jiu-jitsu is made up of many chokes, strangles and holds to the neck. Strengthening the neck will provide some protection against injury while training because the neck will receive a lot of stress. Remember, as with any exercise, to start with what you can do comfortably and progress slowly as you get stronger and your muscles adapt to the exercise.

The Technique

Lie down with both knees raised but your feet on the floor. Push your hips up towards the ceiling so that your body weight is supported only by your head and your feet. Now, carefully turn your head to one side, carefully turn it back to the middle and then carefully to the other side.

Remember this is a sport-specific training drill to improve your performance in Brazilian jiu-jitsu. This should not be done if you have any neck problems and should be stopped immediately if you get any neck pain. If you wish to modify the drill so that you can start at a lower level and work your way up you can do adopt the following: lie down on your back and put both hands on your chest. Bring your

Neck drill.

Weight on head.

Move to both sides.

Standing drill.

Pull left leg behind.

chin down to touch your chest and then put your head back on to the floor. You are using your neck to lift your head up down. You should work at this drill until you can do a hundred repetitions. Be sure you work up to this number rather than try and do it from the start and thus risk injuring yourself before you have even started; begin with twenty repetitions and work up to a hundred.

Standing Drill

Initially this move may look like a technical or complicated method of standing up from sitting on the floor. However, it does have important applications as the principle of it is to regain your feet without leaving yourself vulnerable from an opponent looking to attack you from the standing position. This movement is used a lot in Brazilian jiu-jitsu and is often continued on into a sweep or take-down, but the technique is also common in mixed martial arts competitions or vale tudo competitions. Remember — Brazilian jiu-jitsu was developed in the streets, fighting for money against all styles of fighting. Many of the techniques you will learn have not just been developed so that you can fight other Brazilian jiu-jitsu fighters but so that such fighters are also effective against other styles. This technique was developed for the fighter who is on the floor when his opponent is standing up. It was developed so the fighter can stand up and protect himself

Right arm protects the head.

Finish standing.

from the kicks and punches the opponent is going to try and hit him with.

The Technique

While you are seated on the floor, turn your hips to the right with your left leg bent and the right one relaxed. Lean slightly back so that your body weight is supported by the right leg and the left arm. The right arm is held in front of your face for protection. To stand up, put your weight on the right leg and then pass your left leg between your right leg and left arm in a sweeping motion, placing your right foot behind you. Your knees should be slightly bent and you should remain leaning forward, ready to attack, with your left arm still raised to protect your face.

Sprawl

The sprawl is a technique for defending yourself against an opponent who is attempting to take you to the floor, using either a single or a double-leg take-down (see Chapter 3). The defence is simple but effective. As the attacker dives in to take your legs, you drop your chest on to his back, driving your opponent to the floor. The single or double-leg take-downs are some of the most common in Brazilian jiu-jitsu and so it important to develop a defence to these attacks that is fast and becomes second nature. As you develop this technique it is important that you also develop the drill to be able to sprawl as fast as you can and get back to your

Sprawl.

Drop to the floor.

feet as quickly as possible. This should be done repeatedly for a timed period so that you not only improve the technique but also work on your fitness.

The Technique

From a standing position you will sprawl to the floor as fast as you can. To do this drop your body to the floor, supporting your weight through your arms. As you drop kick your legs out behind you and position your body so that one leg is straight behind you and the other is off to one side; your weight will be distributed through your arms and hips. This drill is usually done well into the warm up so that you can really work on your fitness. The instructor will get the students to work in 3min rounds, running on the spot until he shouts Sprawl!, when the students will sprawl as quickly as possible and then stand up as quickly as possible.

Throw legs behind.

Finishing position.

Sit up and thrust drill.

Sit up.

The Sit Up and Thrust Drill

This drill is a fundamental move in your Brazilian jiu-jitsu game because you will use this move to finish many of the different sweeps that you will learn.

The Technique
Start seated, with the right leg bent and the left foot on the floor. Your right leg should be bent and tucked in tightly to your body. You move forwards by thrusting your hips forward and transferring your weight on to the left foot. You may need to put this foot forward a little as you start the movement so that you do not lose your balance when you go forward. Now your body weight is on the left leg. If you have any problem with your knees, you should be careful when

Push hips forward.

doing this movement. If the drill hurts the joints do not do it without consulting a doctor, but if your muscles are sore because they are weak then the drill will strengthen them.

Final Comments

If you want to be a good Brazilian jiu-jitsu fighter, giving proper attention to the warm up is essential so that you can develop the flexibility, strength and stamina necessary to be effective on the mat. However, never forget good technique must always come first, and the warm up drills described above are designed to develop good technique. If you are training and you are stronger than your partner you should not just use brute strength to win, because you will not thereby develop good technique and there is always someone bigger and stronger just around the corner. Try to rely on technique, not strength, if you are sparring with somebody smaller than you. It does not matter if you fail in executing a technique in sparring since the most important thing is that you learn how to apply it with the minimum of effort and strength. If your movements are smooth and fast then you have the basis to develop the perfect combination of good technique and strength.

3   Take-Downs

Brazilian jiu-jitsu is designed so that a smaller man can fight and defeat one who is larger and stronger. In it a fighter does not want to trade punches and kicks with a much stronger adversary. Instead, the primary aim is to get your opponent to the floor so that you can then use the unique Brazilian jiu-jitsu skills shown here to beat him. This makes the take-downs of primary importance, because the sooner you get the opponent to the floor, the less time he has to damage you and the quicker you can use these unique skills to finish the fight.

In a Brazilian jiu-jitsu competition you will always start in the stand-up position and so it is important that you should try to dominate your opponent from the take-down. A good take-down will give you a positional advantage over your opponent and win you precious points. If you want to fight in competitions you will need to develop good take-down skills since these could well give you the edge you need to win close fights. Normally, in a class the students will start sparring from the kneeling position. Obviously the take-down is important, but for a Brazilian jiu-jitsu fighter the most important moves and techniques are the ones used on the floor to gain a submission. Take-downs are important because they can give you a potentially winning advantage at the start of a fight, but a good take-down is not a guarantee of victory. If you get thrown and your opponent achieves a successful take-down he will get some points, but it will not be the end of the fight. This will continue for the allotted time or until one of the fighters gets a submission. If you are skilled, and patient, you will get your chance at some point to finish the fight. Brazilian jiu-jitsu emphasizes ground fighting and most fighters will want to take the fight to the ground as quickly as possible, particularly if they are fighting stand-up fighters from another martial art.

You will need a partner with whom to practise these moves. To train hard for a competition it is best that you choose a partner with a similar body weight to your own, because in competition fighters are divided into categories according to weight. However, when you are learning and sparring you should practise with people some of whom are heavier and others lighter. Only then will you develop to your true potential and be able to adjust your approach to different opponents. Try to do all moves many times so they become second nature. These techniques will not work if you do not do them correctly and follow the instructions step by step. Take your time in learning them. You will most likely experience some problems and difficulties in the beginning. This is normal and to be expected. Do not worry because after regular practice these complex moves will become smooth and you will develop your personal Brazilian jiu-jitsu game, choosing the best take-downs, submissions and holds that work for you.

Double leg take-down.

Right knee forward.

Double Leg Take-down

This is a common take-down in Brazilian jiu-jitsu. It is fast, direct and very effective. You will find some variations to it but it is not a complex move. Pay attention to detail and concentrate on making the move second nature. This is any aggressive move where the fighter is looking to take control and dominate the fight from the start. However, do not lose control of the move or you will be countered and the move will be quickly turned against you. The defence against this attack was detailed Chapter 2.

The Technique

Stand in front of your partner. Go forward with your right knee so that it is on the floor between your partner s feet. This move is used in no-rules fighting and mixed martial arts fights; the move needs to be fast therefore so that you are safe from kicks and strikes. Next, put your head on your partner s right hip and your shoulder on his stomach so that you knock him off balance. With both palms facing up, put your hands behind both of your partner s knees. Step your left leg to the side of his right leg and use your hands to pull his legs in tight to your body. Now that you have your partner s balance, push him back with your right shoulder and the side of your neck. As you push, try and twist his body to your right and pull his right leg up. By twisting his body to the right and pushing his body to the floor, you should finish in the side mount position (*see* Chapter 7).

Left leg comes forward.

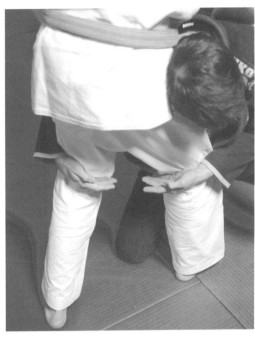

Correct hand position.

Pressure with head on hip.

Stand and lift the leg.

Sprawl Defence

The defence to the attack described above is outlined in Chapter 2 and in more detail here. This defence is an important one to master since it works well, but practice is essential because, you must remember, your opponent will try to make this take-down as fast as possible. It means that your anticipation and reaction time must be good.

The Technique

Your partner is trying to take you down with the double leg take-down, but you are preparing to defend against this attack. You have to sprawl with your chest over your partner s neck and need to put one of your arms underneath his armpit, with the other one over his shoulder and around his body. This allows you to block any attempt by him to get hold of your legs. The arm that is underneath your partner is the one that controls your partner s shoulder. The pressure from your chest will keep his head down, but you must keep your hips down and the pressure of your body weight on the back of your partner s shoulders to maintain control over his body. By controlling one arm you have prevented your opponent from reaching your leg on that side. However, your other leg will be vulnerable to attack. To prevent this you will turn your body, looking over your shoulder on the side which is controlling your opponent s arm. You will then straighten your other leg behind you so that it will be out of his reach.

Single Leg Take-down

The single leg take-down is a technical variation of the double leg take-down and therefore similar to it. However, there are important differences that you need to pay attention to.

Sprawl defence.

Correct position of arms and legs.

Rear view.

Single leg take-down.

Moving forward with the right knee.

Grab the ankle.

Stand with head in opponent's hip.

Trap the leg.

Change the grip.

Step around and apply pressure.

Finish.

The Technique

Stand in front of your partner. Come forward on to your right knee so that it is between your partner s feet. Put your right knee to the side of his right foot and put your head into his right hip. Make sure that you drive your weight right forward. Grab your partner s gi trousers or his leg below the right knee. Slide your left leg around past the outside of his right foot. As you stand, control the leg and keep pressing forward with your head. You are now leaning forward, pushing your partner with your head while holding his right leg, trapping it between your legs. From this position, change your grip on your partner s leg so that your right hand is gripping his thigh and your left leg is near the ankle or the lower leg. Step your left leg around behind you and to the other side of your opponent s leg. At the same time, using your momentum, drive your right shoulder into his leg and force them to the floor. From here you can pass his guard.

Rolling Underneath Your Opponent

This take-down is a difficult technique for a beginner since it a sacrifice technique. Such a technique is one in which you throw yourself to the floor to unbalance and throw your opponent. These throws are highly effective and particularly useful against an experienced opponent who is good at reading and blocking most conventional take-downs. The downside to them is that they are relatively high risk because you are completely committed to the throw and, if your opponent reads it or counters it, you will be in a vulnerable position on the floor. Generally this throw is for a more experienced fighter who has trained for some time and skilled enough to recover his position if he over-commits on the throw.

The Technique

With your left hand, hold your partner s lapel on his right side, grasping the end of your partner s left sleeve with your right hand. Then take one step backwards with your right leg. This is important because it will help to loosen your partner s grip. Stretch his right arm over your left and slide your right leg to your left side. Your partner will feel a lot of pressure on his right arm, as if the shoulder were being twisted forwards in the socket. When you throw your body weight under his arm and behind him this will twist the arm at speed and force him to roll forwards to relieve the pressure and prevent damage to his shoulder and arm. This will bring you to the floor on your right side. As you get to the floor, you will need to change the right grip to the end of the right gi trouser leg of your partner. You should ideally look to finish the move in the side mounted position (*see* Chapter 7).

Rolling take-down.

Step back to apply pressure.

Correct grip.

Pass the leg underneath.

Moving weight down.

Roll body under opponent's arm.

Reverse view.

Finish.

Sweeping or Passing Behind One Leg

This take-down is used frequently because it is disguised by the double leg and the single leg take-down (if you look at the beginning of this take-down it is exactly the same as in them). The moment to use this move is when both you and your opponent are in the clinch (unlike the double and the single leg where you are not engaged with your opponent) with control of the arm and the neck. This position is common in fighting vale tudo as well as in jui-jitsu. Your opponent more often than not will prepare to defend himself from one or the other of these two take-downs. However, you will change the direction of the throw in the middle of the movement to catch him off guard and off balance. This makes your opponent easier to take down and gives you the chance to take advantage of his confusion. This take-down is a useful weapon to have because it is a variation on some of the standard take-downs a Brazilian jiu-jitsu fighter would expect to have used

against him. This expectation sets this throw up nicely for you, and, executed correctly, places you in a dominant position on the floor.

The Technique

You begin this throw by controlling your partner by his neck with your right hand and controlling his sleeve with your left. You push your partner s right arm forward and up at the elbow and put your right knee on the ground. You now sweep forward with your left foot and place it behind your partner. Make sure that your head is tight to your partner s right side. From here, you stand up, twisting to the left with your head tight to his back and keeping firm grip around his in the form of a hug. Note the grip that you use to do this. Push your head to the right so that your partner leans forward, pass your left leg behind his legs and twist his body to the left to break his balance and to protect your head. Use your weight to pull him backwards and your leg to prevent him from stepping backwards. As your partner hits the mat, keep control of his body since you want to

Sweeping leg take-down.

Pass under opponent's grip.

Control from the side.

The nature of reaction force.

Correct grip.

Pass the leg behind.

continue the move to obtain a dominant position on the floor. With your right arm over your partner's chest, put your left hand on the mat to support your body. Bend your right knee and go to the side mount position (see Chapter 7). Make sure that your hips are low to the floor so that your partner cannot turn into you and escape. From this finishing position you have total control over him.

Final Comments

To master these take-downs practice is the key, attention to detail is essential, but it is only with practice that they will become smooth and eventually fast. Remember that in Brazilian jiu-jitsu a fighter does not want to trade punches and kicks with a much stronger adversary in the stand-up position but to get his opponent to the floor as quickly as possible so that he can then use the unique skills described here to finish him and win.

Finish in side mount.

4 The Guard, Variations and Its Submissions

One of the most distinctive positions in Brazilian jiu-jitsu is the guard. In this position you hold your opponent between your legs while you are lying on your back. If your legs are wrapped around his waist and crossed behind his back then the guard is closed . An inexperienced fighter will assume that when he is held in the guard that he has a superior position to you, because he is on top. Yet, by holding the opponent between your legs, it is you who has control over him. Despite being on your back, there are a number of submissions, holds and strikes that can be employed from this position. Used correctly, the guard position allows a much smaller fighter to control, frustrate and finish a much bigger, more aggressive opponent.

There are some important variations from the basic guard position: the spider guard and the butterfly guard position. By using these three you can keep changing your guard position to frustrate your opponent and keep him guessing as to your next move, but, more importantly, allowing you to still keep control over your opponent. These positions will help you to become a good guard user and therefore effective on the floor, because any opponent on top of you will be unable to dominate you and he will waste energy and time in trying to pass your guard. By developing a good technique in these three positions and learning the different submissions that are possible from these three positions you will be able to become an effective fighter from underneath your opponent.

The Basic Guard Position

This position is probably the first one you would learn in any Brazilian jiu-jitsu class. It is a powerful one from which to control and frustrate a larger, stronger opponent who is trying to dominate you. This position is useful when you are under pressure or you have lost control of a fight. It will allow you to regain control if you are in trouble and, if necessary, get a measure of rest before attacking your opponent again. This particular guard position is usually regarded as primarily defensive, but be alert to the possible offensive moves you can apply from the basic guard because it still gives you plenty of attacking options.

The Technique
In this position you hold your opponent between your legs while you are lying on your back. If your legs are wrapped around his waist and crossed behind his back then the guard is closed.

The Butterfly Guard Position

This an important variation on the basic guard since the butterfly guard is a much more attacking position, because you are going to use it to sweep your opponent and therefore gain a much more dominant and threatening position from which to attack. You can usually work yourself into the butterfly guard from the basic guard position or vice versa. It is therefore important that you practise these techniques

Basic guard position.

Butterfly guard.

together and not in isolation. Your ability to flow from one position to another with the minimum of effort will make you a much more effective fighter.

The Technique

Sit directly in front of your opponent and place your feet between his legs with your knees bent. One of your arms passes underneath the arm of your opponent and allows you to take a firm hold of his back. This leaves your other arm free to control his arm. By controlling him in this way you will be able to sweep him. You are going to learn more about how to sweep from this position in Chapter 10. For now, the important thing is that you can comfortably put this position into effect.

The Spider Guard Position

This guard position is the most attacking of the three and therefore the most difficult to execute effectively. You will need to practise this position with a number of partners of differing weight and height. This is because you want to use this position to gain control over your opponent, to break his balance and then manipulate him into the position you want him to be in when you make your attack. As this position is such an attacking one, many of the sweeps, locks, chokes or strangles described here will start from this position. It is one that you will need to work at because many fighters feel vulnerable in it and it requires good control and confidence to execute it effectively. However, once mastered, this position can be used to devastating effect.

The Technique

You control your opponent by holding the sleeves of his gi and firmly putting your feet on the inside of his hips. You then use your knees to put pressure on the inside of his arms. This is important because this pressure means that your opponent no longer has control over his arms. You can then pull him slightly towards you, giving you complete control of his balance. You then have a range of attacking options that are described later in this chapter and elsewhere. For now, the important thing is to practise this position so that you can control your opponent with confidence from it.

Submissions from the Guard

The following moves are some of the ways in which you can finish a fight. The locks, chokes and strangles that are detailed below are those that cause your opponent pain and discomfort and therefore force him to submit. You cause pain and discomfort in applying these techniques because you are threatening the health of your opponent. A lock is applied to a joint of

Spider guard controlling the hips.

Spider guard controlling the arms.

your opponent and, if applied with enough force, will cause ligament damage and fracture. A choke will cut off the air supply to the brain and a strangle will cut off the blood supply to the brain; if applied with enough force both will cause your opponent to pass out. If you continue to keep a choke or a strangle on your opponent after he has passed out then he will die. Given the serious consequences of applying any of these techniques incorrectly, you need to practise them with control and common sense.

Make sure that your partner understands the rule of tapping out : this is a fundamental rule to both Brazilian jiu-jitsu and judo. If you apply any technique that your opponent feels threatens his health he will tap the mat or himself with his hand. You need to be aware of your opponent s tapping and let go immediately if he or a partner taps. This is his way of letting you know that he could be in serious trouble and that you must release him immediately. If you do not you will be held responsible for any harm that you cause. This tapping rule applies in both training and competition; obviously if a fighter taps out in competition then he will lose the fight and you will have caused your opponent to submit. Take care not to injure someone seriously because you did not take notice of his attempts to tap out; if you do not do so in either competition or practice then you will be disqualified from that competition or the club or class that you are training with will expel you. If your opponent cannot tap with his hands then he will use his feet to tap the mat. This rule is fundamental in keeping both practice and competition safe — do not break it.

When you first start to practise these moves you will lack the knowledge to know to what degree they are hurting your opponent. Without his tapping out when he feels discomfort you are not going to get the feedback you need by which to know whether your technique is effective or not. By tapping out at the right time you let your partner know when the technique has been applied properly and you

keep yourself free from injury. One last piece of advice: these techniques work and were designed to maim and cause severe injury. Do not try to resist them with strength and tap out at the last second just as the technique starts to really hurt. I cannot think of a quicker way to injure yourself, and if you do so you cannot train, and if you cannot train you cannot learn and develop. Remember that jiu-jitsu is based on the principle that your opponent is much bigger and stronger than you. Use good technique, not strength, to defeat your opponent. To develop this you must practise again and again with control. Practise the movements slowly until you understand them, speed up only when you and, more importantly, your partner understands what you are both doing. Done properly these techniques do not require any strength to apply them effectively; if you are having to use strength to apply them then you need to re-examine and alter your technique.

It was important to put in these finishing techniques after you have read and understood the guard positions. These are positional techniques, they get you into the position you need to be able to finish the fight. The submission techniques are the ones you use to finish the fight once you are in such a position. One set of techniques is useless without the other, they come as an integrated pair. For example, a boxer could have an incredible punch, a right-hand that will knock any other fighter out, but if he does not have the knowledge and skill to get into a position from which he can throw that punch effectively he will never get to use it. So it is in Brazilian jiu-jitsu: if you do not use the guard positions to work yourself into dominating positions you will never be able to use the submission techniques that are detailed below. A good Brazilian jiu-jitsu fighter is a patient, controlled fighter who will constantly dominate his opponent by gaining and maintaining a good position and therefore control over his opponent s body. Such a fighter will then take his opportunity to finish the fight

Arm lock from the guard.

Control the arm.

quickly and ruthlessly, whether that opportunity comes in the first or the last seconds of a fight. Such a fighter knows that that opportunity will come from gaining and maintaining a good position; if this is achieved, your opponent will eventually give you the opportunity to finish him, however good he is.

The Arm Bar

This is probably the most common submission in Brazilian jiu-jitsu and one of the first techniques you would be taught. The arm bar is an arm lock. It has no respect for size, strength or weight. If you get caught with an arm bar and lack complete confidence in your escape techniques, tap. The arm bar applied correctly, and without your opponent s tapping first, will fracture the elbow joint. It is a lovely technique because it is simple and can be applied from so many different positions. You will get into the position from which to apply it whenever your

opponent begins to straighten his arm, and it is therefore possible to apply whether your opponent is attacking or defending. For example, when he is attacking and trying to apply a choke or defending by trying to escape from the guard, he will tend to straighten his arms, this is gold dust to a Brazilian jiu-jitsu fighter. Many fighters will pretend to try and go for a choke or strangle in the hope that their opponents will defend the move by blocking with an arm. This will give the fighter the control of that arm and therefore make it easier to apply the technique.

The Technique

Hold your opponent s arm with your opposite arm by taking hold of the triceps and snaking your arm over his arm. You pull your opponent s arm towards you and put his elbow against your stomach. You now have control of the arm. You then open your guard and put your foot on your opponent s hip, on the same side that you have his arm. Turn your body

Move your hips to the side

Push the head.

Pass the leg and pull.

Correct arm position with the thumb up.

towards the opposite side of his. This is made easier by hooking the other leg behind your opponent s back; this will prevent your opponent from sitting up and will make the technique much easier to perform. To turn your body to the side you will also use your foot (on the other leg) to push against your opponent s hip. You will then use your other arm to push your opponent s head away from you. This will make the space you need to pass your leg around his head. To do this, you have to lift your hips up by bridging your body and stretching your legs. With the arm of your opponent trapped against your torso and your legs pushing down against his neck and back, you are forcing your opponent s arm to straighten.

Keep pulling down with your legs and pushing your hips up (the elbow is trapped against your pelvis) and your opponent s arm will overextend and fracture at the elbow. Be careful and remember to tap if you are in trouble. Make sure that your opponent s arm is positioned so that the thumb is pointing to the ceiling, this will make sure that the elbow is in the best position for you to apply maximum force.

The Triangle

The triangle is a strangle which cuts off the blood supply to the brain. In Brazilian jiu-jitsu the fighter uses his legs to put pressure against the neck. This prevents blood from flowing

The triangle.

Pass the leg and pull the arm.

freely through the major arteries and veins of the neck and therefore hinders the supply to the brain. With a lock the pain is immediate, but with a choke or a strangle there is an approximate delay of 6 to 8sec before the technique causes an opponent to pass out. Be careful, because an inexperienced fighter may not realize that a strangle is on until he starts to feel faint, and then he might panic and forget to tap before passing out. Take your time and develop your application of the technique slowly. The degree of pressure you apply to your opponent s neck is dependent upon how hard you squeeze with your legs. This gives you an excellent control of the strangle and of how hard you want to apply it. But there is no excuse for an opponent s or partner s passing out by mistake, you should

have complete control of the technique throughout. This technique is particularly popular with Brazilian jiu-jitsu fighters when they are on the floor and underneath their opponent. Try and apply the technique from the basic guard and the spider guard position. It will provide you with a useful attacking option when you are in either of these positions and make you a much more dangerous fighter from below. The technical description is given below, but your own flexibility will determine the precise mechanics of the move for you. Remember: if you have to use strength to apply this technique you are not doing it properly. Go back to the technical detail and refine the move until you can apply it effortlessly. In the description below you are going to work the triangle from the spider guard so

Close the triangle.

Reverse view.

Pull the head to finish.

that you can get into good habits straightaway and learn the positional and finishing techniques in sequence and not in isolation.

The Technique

Place your partner in the spider guard, making sure that your feet are on the inside of the elbows and that your hands have a firm hold of his sleeves. Start to turn your body and pull with one hand so that you break your partner's balance. He will try to regain his balance by moving back towards the centre. That is the time at which to slide one leg over his shoulder and then the other one under his opposite shoulder. The leg that has passed over his shoulder now snakes around behind his neck. To do this smoothly, you will need to turn your body so that you are at almost 90 degrees to his head. Your leg is now behind his neck and you can look straight at his ear. This leaves one arm between your legs. Keep a tight grip and bring your other leg up and over the shin of the leg behind your partner's neck, just above your foot. To close the triangle simply tighten your leg around the shin of the other leg and turn your body a little further. To finish the move against a stubborn opponent you can pull his head down towards you, tightening the strangle.

The omoplata.

The omoplata.

The Omoplata

This move is called the omoplata because that is the Brazilian name for the shoulder bone and this technique is a shoulder lock. The move is difficult because it requires good timing on your part, and a good understanding of how to break your partner s balance. You will therefore need an understanding partner and patience because you are going to have to practise this move extensively before you master it. The rewards are worth it because the move is diffi-cult to defend against and gives you complete control over your opponent s body.

The omoplata.

The Technique

Place your partner in the full guard. You push one arm back and put your knee under his armpit. Turn your body so that you have an angle to pass your leg around his back (if you take his right arm, angle your body to your left). You then need to sit by his side, with your leg hooked behind his arm. As you sit up, the leg hooked behind the arm will drive your partner forward into the floor. You need to keep a grip of his back with one arm to stop him from rolling, and the other arm needs to keep hold of his sleeve so that you maintain control of his arm. Your partner s forearm is now against your stomach; as you lean forward the pres-sure of your body against his arm makes the lock come on to the shoulder joint.

The omoplata.

Sit up and move hips to side away from opponent's body.

Bend the leg to maintain control.

Sit forward to finish.

The choke from the guard.

Left hand, opposite lapel.

The Choke Using the Opponent s Gi

This is a simple technique and, as a result, many do not really value it. This is a mistake because the move works and can be applied from many different positions. It can be applied from a dominating position when you are on top of an opponent or when you have him in the basic guard and you are underneath him. Never underestimate the effectiveness of a choke: one of pieces of advice my first judo instructor Harry Knowles gave me was that you can break a man s arm, his neck or his leg but he can still fight, but take away his air and it does not matter how big or strong he is, he will not be able to.

The Technique

Place your partner in the basic guard position and cross your legs so that the guard is closed. Place your hand palm up underneath the collar of his gi and drive the hand as deep as possible. It is important that your hand is on the opposite side of your partner s neck so that your arm crosses his body. Your fingers are inside the collar of the gi but your thumb is outside the collar. This gives you a good grip. You then do exactly the same with the other hand on

Correct grip with thumb out.

the other side of your partner s body. Make sure that you have a really deep grip and then simply pull down on his gi and open your elbows outwards. This will pull his head forwards toward you and drive the blade of your forearms against his neck. This will cut off his air supply and will force him to submit.

Pull forward to finish.

Same grip on the other side.

Final Comments

The aim of this chapter has been to introduce you to the guard positions and the possible finishing techniques that you can employ from them. The guard positions are important because they will help you to gain control over your opponent. These are the positions you will look to achieve at the start of a fight or if you are in trouble and under pressure during it. However, the guard positions are only the starting point and it would be a mistake to think that all you have to do is gain the position and then apply a finishing technique to win. The guard positions give you options and, as you become more experienced, you will become more skilled at exploiting these to

your advantage. An experienced Brazilian jiu-jitsu fighter is not just going to let you submit him from the guard position, you are going to have to work to get the position, to keep it and then to finish or sweep from it. It is vital that you learn to flow effortlessly from one position to another and to work patiently. If you cannot find a finish in one position, use your positional skills to gain another from which to attack. The positional and finishing techniques that you learn here come as an integrated set of skills. Try and replicate this in your training, start with individual techniques and positions and master them, but then try to practise them as a set of skills. Whenever you practise a position, look and use the different finishing techniques that you can employ, but whenever you practise a finishing technique also look at the positions that you can move back into if the technique does not go according to plan. Few fights do so and you need to be able to react quickly and effectively to different situations and problems as they arise. You will be able to do this only if you can move swiftly and effectively from one position to another, always alert to the different opportunities to finish the fight that will inevitably come with each.

5 The Half Guard, How to Pass It and Submissions from It

The last chapter covered the guard positions and how to employ them during a fight to either gain and maintain dominant positions or to finish your opponent. The guard positions are a fundamental part of being a good Brazilian jiu-jitsu fighter. Your opponent will therefore work hard to deny you the opportunity to gain and exploit them. As a result, fights do not always follow a perfect plan and often you will get in to a position where your legs are locked around only one of your opponent s legs instead of two. This position is known as the half guard and, as you get better and your opponents more skilful, you will spend more and more time in it. The half guard will provide the opportunity for both fighters to go on and win. Your skill and confidence in this position is crucial to how effective you are as a fighter, because both you and your opponent can turn it to advantage. As a result, fighting in the half guard position is highly tactical and it is one that you do not want to make mistakes in. You will need to practise this position repeatedly.

The half guard is a position that a lot of Brazilian Jiu-jitsu fighters prefer to sweep from, and we shall go in to more detail on this in Chapter 10. However, it is important that you can adapt and that you start to develop a range of skills from the half guard position, otherwise you will become a predictable fighter. In this chapter we are going to concentrate on two main situations: when you have your opponent in the half guard position and when your opponent has you in it. When you have the half guard position you will be on the bottom, and if you can get control of your opponent s balance in

this position you will have the opportunity to attack him and either finish him or gain a more dominant position. When you are caught in the half guard position you will normally try to pass your opponent s half guard, but it is also possible to submit him from it. The important point is that you must not let your opponent gain control over your balance or base, as it is referred to. If you can stabilize your position and keep control over your balance first, you will then gain the control you need to ensure that you are not swept and it will be you who has the opportunity to go on the attack and get a submission or a more dominant position. As you can now see, the half guard is analogous to a game of cat and mouse, with each fighter working to control the other and gain the upper hand. If two fighters are locked in the half guard position there are two likely outcomes:

1. The fighter locked in the half guard will attempt a finishing technique while still locked in it, or pass his opponent s half guard and gain a better position from where to finish the fight.
2. The fighter with the half guard will attempt a finishing technique while his opponent is still locked in the half guard, or he will sweep his opponent and gain a better position from where to finish the fight.

A good Brazilian jiu-jitsu fighter will be highly skilled at both, and this chapter will cover the unique skills required to do both from this common position.

When You Have the Half Guard Position

In this position you are on the bottom, and to most people this will seem to be a position of disadvantage. However, you will know by now that Brazilian jiu-jitsu fighters are quite comfortable on the bottom and that the guard positions were designed to give fighters on the bottom the means with which to attack and dominate their opponents. Many fighters like this position and, when you know how to use it, you will view the half guard as a strong position, one that gives you plenty of opportunity to sweep, defend and finish. However, it does take time to adapt to it and in the beginning you will find it difficult to maintain and develop. You need to persevere since you will need to practise the position a great deal in sparring before you have the skill and confidence to use it in competition. Most people, when they learn Brazilian jiu-jitsu, normally just want to gain the top position (the mount) and dominate their opponent. This is understandable when you begin, but tactically it is oversimplified and unrealistic as you progress and come up against good opponents. The half guard offers your opponent the opportunity to pass your guard and this makes the position more vulnerable than the other guard positions, but it also puts your opponent in a much more vulnerable position. If your opponent attacks you will have the opportunity to counter, and if your opponent does nothing you will have the opportunity to take control of the fight. Whatever happens, try not to freeze in the half guard position. The half guard gives you some control over your opponent and the platform from which to attack. The technique below is an example of how you can turn the half guard into an attack.

The half guard.

Control the hip.

Body is always on the side.

Reverse view.

The Technique

You have the half guard because you are on the bottom with your legs closed around one leg of your partner. It is vital that you never let your partner get control over your shoulders. You must make sure that during the whole time you are in this position that you drop your hips to the side and make a good grab under his arm. Twist your body on to your right side and wrap your left arm around his hip. Never let your partner put his body weight on you since he will then be able to push your back flat on the mat. If this happens you are in real trouble and your partner would have the position he would need to pass your half guard. Therefore keep your head and your shoulder on your partner s chest and your right hand on his knee so that he cannot push your back on to the floor, and try to pull his leg out of your half guard. To continue the movement push your partner s knee back with your right hand and push his buttocks with your left knee. This helps you to twist your hips and escape from underneath him, as well as

helping you take his balance. As you turn, your partner will fall forwards and you will have the space to come up and around him. Remember that it is an important point that you use your partner s strength and balance to execute the movement.

When You Are in the Half Guard Position

Your priority when you are caught in the half guard position is to break and pass the half guard so that you can obtain a much more dominant position or submit your opponent. The break and pass described below is the most common manoeuvre, but, of course, there are variations. But for now we shall stick to basics. If you are trapped in the half guard position try not to panic and use strength to escape because this will give your opponent the control he needs to pass you. If you relax and use good technique it is possible for you to control him, but you need to be careful and do this well because you are in a potentially vulnerable position. Learn

Escape from the half guard.

Stand up.

the basic escape and pass first, the variations will come with time, but only if and when you have learnt the basics well.

The Technique

To get and keep control of your partner when you are trapped in the half guard you must start by keeping his back completely flat to the mat since this will prevent his turning his hips. To do this, control your partner s shoulder by putting your right arm underneath his left arm. You then hold his collar by the neck, drop your body weight to your left side and put your head on the mat by the side of his head, driving your shoulder under his chin. Your left arm must pull tightly on your partner s right arm, keeping his right arm to the left side of your ribs. In this position you are the one who has control over opponent, and now you can make your move. First make sure that your base is good and that you have good control over your balance. Once your position is stable, you pull hard with your right leg so that the leg slips out of the half guard, and

Both arms controlled.

you can now pass to a more dominant position such as the side mount. Clearly this will not be easy and sometimes bouncing up and down on your trapped leg will help to loosen your opponent s grip and allow you to pull your leg free. Always keep control over his shoulders,

Pass the knee.

Finish in control.

keeping his back flat on the floor. Be careful when you are in this position and be sure to keep your weight to the left side since this will prevent your partner from pulling you towards your right side, thereby gaining control over your balance and rolling you over.

Submitting Your Opponent when You Have the Half Guard Position

As mentioned earlier, many Brazilian jiu-jitsu fighters like to sweep from the half guard, but the half guard can offer you some excellent opportunities to finish the fight without having to gain a different position. As you improve, you will develop a range of possible submission techniques from this position; but a word of warning: it is better that you can use three or four techniques really well than ten or fifteen poorly. The half guard offers opportunities to both fighters and it is not a position that you want to make mistakes in. Make sure that the techniques

you develop from the half guard are smooth and well executed, so that you are confident and comfortable.

The Kimura

The kimura is a shoulder lock and one of my favourites. This lock can be applied from the basic guard position and the half guard position. This is worth remembering because often you will lose the basic guard but manage to keep the half guard position. Of course, the reverse is also possible, with your using the half guard position to move into the basic guard. Brazilian jiu-jitsu is about flow and constantly moving from one position to another in order to confuse and unbalance the opponent. As I have said before, these techniques do not come as separate techniques but as an integrated set. The advantage of this lock is that you can use it from two guard positions, therefore you can attack your opponent with it when he is distracted and is least expecting it. If your opponent is focused on your moving from the basic guard position to the half

Kimura from half guard.

Holding the wrist.

Grab your own wrist.

Twist the shoulder.

guard, he is less likely to be aware of your setting him up for the kimura.

The Technique

As your partner is trying to pass your half guard you must turn your body and, most importantly, your hips to the side. Never lie down flat on the floor because, if that happens, you will be in trouble and your opponent will gain control over your shoulders. When you turn your body to one side you will unbalance your partner and he will put his left hand on the floor in an attempt to regain balance. As he tries to do this

and re-establish a good base you will attack his arm. With your left hand you are going to hold his right wrist and keep his right hand on the floor. Pass your right arm around your partner s right and then hold your left wrist with your right hand. You then drive your partner s head into the mat by moving your hips to your left side and pushing your partner s right arm up and behind his back. The lock is now firmly on. Remember that you will always need to keep your partner s leg tight in the half guard to keep control of the movement and prevent him from rolling out of the lock.

59

Choke from the half guard.

Control the arm.

Submitting Your Opponent when You Pass the Half Guard

Your skill and ability to pass the half guard and attack your opponent will determine the amount of pressure you can put him under when you are caught in the half guard position. The more pressure you can exert the more likely your opponent is to panic, make a mistake and give you the opportunity to finish the fight. Whenever you are trying to pass the half guard, trying to get into a better position, you should pay attention to any opportunity that may arise to submit your opponent. It does not matter which submission technique you use so long as you are effective. There are many possible techniques you can employ if you get control of your opponent s body first. But you have to be careful when you are passing the half guard because if you do not have control

first your opponent is going to sweep or submit you. There are many fighters in Brazilian jiu-jitsu who are skilled, confident and effective in the guard and the half guard position and they will make it as difficult as possible for you to pass their guard. So you must practise how to pass the guard and the half guard position over and over again until you are able to do it with skill, confidence and speed.

The Technique
When you are caught in the half guard position your first priority is to break and pass it, keeping control of the position at all times. However, this time you will not get control of your partner by holding under his arm. Instead, you will pass your right arm up and around the back of his neck. You are using your right arm because it is your right leg that is caught in your partner s half guard. Take your

Take the hold.

Hips up.

Pass the guard.

Finish with the choke.

partner s right arm and pass the arm to his left side, pushing it across his neck so that the biceps is on the throat with pressure. You then use your head to keep his right arm in place across his neck. Place your right hand on the left biceps and your left hand on his head. From this position you can apply great pressure. Maintain a good base so that you can lift your hips up and pull your right leg out of the half guard. If your partner has a strong grip on your leg in the half guard you can use your left foot to help you to pull your right leg out. With your right leg free you can pass your partner s guard, bringing your right leg down on the same side of his body as your left leg. Lean into your partner so that you are pushing his arm on to his neck. This will choke him and give you the submission.

Final Comments

To be really effective in the half guard position you must practise. A good drill with which to practise this position is to put your partner in the half guard and let him try and pass your half guard, without your trying to finish him. Instead, work at trying to unbalance him in this position so that he never gains the balance he needs to get control over your body to pass your half guard. When you have done this, change over so that you are now in your partner s half guard and work at trying to pass it without finishing your partner. Try to pass the half guard and find a more dominant position from which you would attack. What is important here is that you work at keeping a good balance. With this good base you can work on the techniques that you need to refine to get control over your opponent s body. The half guard will provide both fighters with the opportunity to take control of the fight. You need to be able to react and deal with the different attacks, feints and sweeps that are common to this position. As always, practice is the key. The half guard is a highly tactical position, and you must be comfortable in it to be able to exploit the opportunities that will inevitably come your way. If you panic and try to use strength to dominate then a skilful opponent will exploit this and gain the upper hand. You will need to be patient and use skill, good technique and work hard to turn this position to your advantage.

6 Passing the Guard

In Chapter 4 we looked at the different guard positions that you can use to gain control of your opponent and in Chapter 5 we looked at an important variation to the basic guard position, the half guard position, and how you can use it to your advantage. The guard positions are such a central part of Brazilian jiu-jitsu that you will spend much of your time either trying to get your opponent into your guard or trying to break out of his guard. Due to the difficulty of attacking an opponent who has you in the guard, it is best, if you are caught in your opponent s guard, to break out of it and get into a better position from where you can more effectively attack him.

The task of breaking out of your opponent s guard and passing around his legs to attain a better position is known as passing the guard. It is a crucial skill for any fighter to master because your ability to attain a better position from which to dominate and submit a fighter is fundamental in winning a fight. The guard positions were developed so that you can defend yourself against your opponent s attacks, gain control of his balance and then attack him. You do not want to spend time in your opponent s guard. If you find yourself so caught during a fight and you are unable to break his guard and pass you are going to be in serious trouble. It is possible to apply some submission techniques (some foot locks and leg locks) when caught in your opponent s guard, but they are difficult to do and you will have little control over your opponent, making them high risk techniques to attempt in competition. If you are caught

in your opponent s guard your priority must be to break it, pass the guard and attain a better position from which to attack.

If you are caught in your opponent s basic guard, so that you are fighting from the top position, and manage to pass it you will not only gain a better position from which to attack but in competition you will also gain three points. This is a recognition of the fact that passing the guard is difficult against a skilled opponent. You are going to have work at these passing techniques if you are going to be effective. Your opponent does not want you to pass his guard because if you do it is he who has lost control of the fight. Your opponent will therefore do everything he can to prevent this. You will need good technique in this position because you will not be able to break your opponent s guard with brute strength and you do want to waste valuable energy in a long fight, constantly struggling to break free from his guard.

There are many ways to pass the guard and you can do so from a variety of positions. For example, you can pass the guard from a standing or a kneeling position. In fact, your ability to change from one position to another while you constantly attack your opponent s guard, will help you to confuse and distract him and this will help you to break his guard. When you are learning your passing techniques you will inevitably develop some favourites. Certain techniques are easier for certain people, depending on their flexibility and body shape, but also some techniques will be better suited against certain opponents because of their flexibility and body shape. It is therefore important that you should learn and develop more than just one or two techniques to pass the guard and also important that those you do learn can be put into practice on both your left and your right side. A skilful opponent is not going to give you many opportunities to pass his guard and, if you have worked hard to develop an opportunity to pass, you need to be able to take advantage of them straightaway. Always work hard on your weaknesses, and to learn a technique for both the right and the left side will make you a better fighter because you are better prepared to take advantage of opportunities as they arise. A valuable piece advice I was given by my first judo instructor was that, if you are practising a technique on the left and the right side and one is better than the other, then you should increase your training on the weaker side. So if your right side is the stronger, then every time you practise the technique on your right you should practise the same technique twice on your left side. This will help you to become skilled and confident on both sides and therefore a much more balanced and better fighter.

Breaking and Passing the Guard

Always remember that you are vulnerable to the sweep if you are locked in your opponent s guard. It is therefore of vital importance that, if you are going to attack his guard, from whatever position, that you have and maintain a good base. If you have a good base, then your opponent is going to find it difficult to sweep and you will be in a much better position to put the pressure you need to exert on to your opponent s body and therefore to gain control of the situation. To open an opponent s guard you must be able to gain and keep control of his body.

From Kneeling

This particular technique for breaking and passing the guard is a very common one because it is so effective. It is also usual that, if your opponent has you in his guard, you will probably be on your knees because your opponent will be trying to get you to the floor to sweep and dominate you. Grasp the top of your opponent s trousers and push down, forcing his hips to the floor. Then bring your elbows inside, digging them into the top of your opponent s thighs. This is extremely uncomfortable and virtually impossible for your opponent to resist for any length of time. Place one knee at the base of your opponent s spine while sitting back on your other knee. This applies more pressure on the legs, while also preventing any movement and giving you maximum control. This, when done correctly, will apply enough pressure to open the guard. When you have just opened the guard it is absolutely vital that you keep control of your partner s body; if you do not, your partner is simply going to turn his hips to the side, regain control over his legs and put you straight back in the guard. You may have broken your partner s guard but you must still work hard, with good control, to pass it. Pass one leg (in this case the left) over his right leg, across the thigh, stopping with your knee and your foot touching the floor, therefore pinning the leg. Your left arm must come up and around your partner s neck, as if you were trying to hug him, getting a good grip, since it is this pressure that gives you control of your partner s chest. Then your right arm must take a grip on your partner s left leg at about knee level. Be careful if you do not have a strong grip on the left leg because your opponent still has the opportunity to trap you in the half guard. To get and keep control over the position you must use your chest to put as much pressure as possible on your opponent s chest, thereby keeping him firmly against the mat. This gives you that vital control over your partner s body and will prevent his escaping from the pass. You

Elbows inside.

Reverse view.

Apply pressure.

Change your base.

Open the guard.

Pass the leg over.

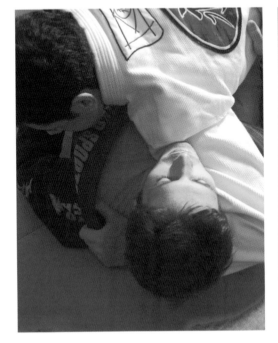

The correct grip.

Pass the other leg.

Finish in side
mount.

are then going to pull your right leg around behind you and drive your knee firmly against the side of your partner s hips. This will prevent him from turning. Now pull the right leg around and behind you. Keep this leg stretched out behind you to give you a good base. You are now in what is called the side mount position in Brazilian jiu-jitsu, a good one from which to dominate and attack your partner. Remember that you must always keep a good base when you are opening the guard.

From Standing Up

Another way to break and pass the guard is when you stand up. Start from the same kneeling position as before; as always with passing the guard, make sure that you have a good base. You then have to get control over one of your partner s hands, it does not matter which hand so long as the arm you are trying to control is on the same side of your body as the arm you are using. In the pictures you are

controlling your partner s right arm with your left hand. You then put his arm on his stomach, but always keep pushing his hips down. This will prevent your partner from being able to move or turn. Now stand up and step your left leg out to the same side as that on which you are holding your partner s arm. You must step on the same side as the arm you have trapped because, if you step around with the other leg, your opponent will have the chance to take you down by gripping your leg with his free arm. You now push his left leg down towards the mat until his leg passes below your knee. This allows you to bend your leg and put pressure over your partner s leg, as you did with the kneeling technique. You need to bend your leg until your knee touches the floor and pins your partner s leg to the floor. This means, as before, that your shin is running across your partner s leg and keeping it pinned tightly to the floor. Your right arm must come up and around your partner s neck with a good grip, so that you have control

Passing the guard from standing.

Control the arm and stand.

Push the knee.

Pass the knee over.

Control the body.

Pass the guard.

Reverse view.

Finish in side mount.

Passing the open guard.

Control the legs and push.

of your partner s chest. Then your left arm must take a grip on his right leg, at about knee level. To get and keep control over the position you must use your chest to put as much pressure as possible on your partner s chest, thereby keeping his back firmly against the mat. You then are going to pull your left leg around behind you and drive your knee firmly against the side of his hips. This will prevent your opponent from turning. Then pull the right leg around and behind you. Keep this leg stretched out behind you to give you a good base. You are now in the side mount position again.

When You Are Standing but Your Opponent Is on the Floor

This position is more common in Brazilian jiu-jitsu than most people realize at first. What tends to happen is that a fighter has just opened the opponent s guard, but has lost control of the movement and is unsure about passing. The fighter will stand up to move away from his opponent, to stop him from countering the initial attack and attacking him. In this position one fighter is still lying on his back while the

other is now standing up. But the fighter who is standing still has the same problem. He may have broken his opponent s guard but he has not passed it. The fighter standing up still needs to get around his opponent s legs so that he can really attack his opponent. This position is common in mixed martial arts competitions where a fighter has broken the guard and stood up because he wants to fight standing and not on the floor. However, in Brazilian jiu-jitsu you want to be on the floor but not in your opponent s guard, so you must be able to pass around your opponent s legs so that you can attack him from the side or from on top.

This move starts with your partner lying down, with his guard open, and with you standing, ready to try passing his guard. As always when you pass the guard, maintain a good base. When you are in this position never let your opponent get control over your sleeves because if your partner does you will be in the spider guard and your partner will sweep you. First, you have to get a good grip on the end of your partner s trousers. You then push his legs towards his head and

Step to one side.

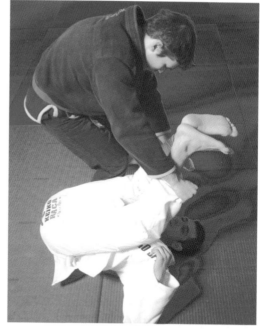

Maintain pressure.

Reverse view.

Pass to knee on belly.

keep pushing down on his lower back so that you are exerting considerable pressure on him and therefore controlling his body. At the same time, you have to place your right foot by his right hip, keeping as close to his body as possible. Now turn your body in towards your partner and drive your right knee down on to his stomach. Your left leg will naturally step around behind you and help you to drive your right knee down into your partner. You now have what is called the knee-on-the-belly position in Brazilian jiu-jitsu. To stabilize the position properly you must hold your opponent s gi behind his neck with your left hand, and your right hand needs to be holding his knee or belt on his left side.

Final Comments

No fight ever goes exactly to plan and in some you are going to find yourself in trouble. If you are caught in your opponent s guard your priority must be to break it, pass the guard and attain and maintain a dominant position over your opponent as quickly as possible. You need to practise breaking and passing the guard with your partner over and over again because your ability to break and pass the guard will have a huge influence on your ability to dominate and to win fights. Remember that you must establish a really good base before breaking and passing the guard, otherwise your opponent will sweep and finish you. When you train with your partner work on breaking the guard by letting him put you in the guard and you try to escape. As soon as you do so go back into his guard and do the same thing all over again. Keep doing this so that you become reliant on good technique and not brute strength to open and pass the guard. If you are in a competition and your opponent is ahead on points as you come to the end of a long and hard fight your opponent will try and trap you in the basic guard position to gain control over you to prevent you from attacking him and wind down the clock until the end of the fight. You will not turn this situation around, pass the guard and win if you try and use brute strength to dominate your opponent, you will simply be too tired and weak and be playing straight into his hands. You are going to need good technique and to be cunning.

7 The Side Mounted Position, Variations and Their Arm Bar Submissions

The side mounted position is a powerful one from which you can and should dominate and finish your opponent. If you gain this position you have done the hard work of passing your opponent s guard, applying a good take-down to your opponent or sweeping him from one of the guard positions. If you know how to stabilize and control the side mounted position it is a bad one for your opponent to be in. When you apply this technique properly, your opponent (who is on the bottom) is under huge pressure because it is you who has control over his body. You have so many other dominating positions that you can move in and out of with complete control, such as the knee-on-the-belly, the north—south position (also known as upper four quarters in judo and the sixty-nine position in Brazilian jiu-jitsu) and the mounted position.

Remember, Brazilian jiu-jitsu is about movement that flows, so a fighter does not gain a dominant position just to hold it. He is going to look to exploit it by moving between different dominant positions so that he can confuse and distract his opponent and engineer an opening for the finish. This is a major difference between judo and Brazilian jiu-jitsu — a judo fighter can catch an opponent in the side mounted position and, if he holds his opponent in this position for 30sec, he will win the fight. As a result, a judo fighter is limited in his application of this technique because all he is looking to do is just to keep the hold on for this period. In contrast, the Brazilian jiu-jitsu fighter is looking to the side mounted position as an opportunity to dominate and finish his opponent. The fighter will get three points for being able to get to the side mounted position, but no more. Unlike the judo fighter, the Brazilian jiu-jitsu fighter must use this position to move on and keep trying to accumulate more points or to win by submission. He does not have the option of using this position to close down the fight in the same way that a judo fighter does. It is this pressure to push techniques constantly to a clear win or submission that has meant that Brazilian jiu-jitsu has evolved into a much more complex and comprehensive fighting art on the floor than judo has. While a judo fighter will just look to hold certain positions, a Brazilian jiu-jitsu fighter will use the side mounted position to go direct for a submission or another dominating position.

The Side Mounted Position

It is important that when you apply this position you maintain good control over your opponent s body. Remember: your opponent is in a bad position and will be working hard to escape. He is going to try and escape more often than not by turning in towards you and trying to trap you in his guard. Pay attention to the use of your hips, because, if you do not keep them down, you will be unable to control his hips and he will then be able to turn.

The side mount.

Reverse view.

The Technique

Your partner is lying down on his back. You approach from the side and place your chest on top of your partner s chest direct. The downwards pressure of your body through his chest will give you control of his upper body and keep his back on the mat. If you approach your partner from his right side, your left arm will snake around the back of his neck and hold his gi. Your right arm will hold just under his left arm. You must also drive your left knee against the side of his hips. This is important because it will stop your partner from turning his hips and trapping you in one of the guard positions. With your left leg bent, you push your right leg out behind you to give you a good base. Remember that you have to keep pushing your hips down and the knee nearer to your partner s legs tight against his hips in order to control them. This control of the hips, coupled with the downward pressure you are putting on your partner s chest with your chest, will give you the control you need to keep your partner firmly pinned to the mat.

The Americana

This is a shoulder lock and a simple but effective submission technique that can be used whether your opponent is wearing a gi or not. When you first learn this technique you will normally do so from the side mounted position, but bear in mind that this technique can be applied from other positions as well, such as the mounted position.

The Technique

Put your partner in the side mounted position and stabilize your position by keeping your hips pushed down and your leg bent and tight to the side of your partner s hips. Keep your chest pushed down on his chest and maintain your balance. Do not let your partner shift your weight to either side of his body. This will prevent your opponent from turning and escaping. To attack his right arm you will need to force it to the floor by his head. Use your left hand to pin your partner s left wrist to the floor. Your right hand, which is under his arm, moves up and takes hold of your left wrist. Keep your partner s wrist

The Americana.

Grab the wrist.

Pass your arm under.

Pull the elbow up and towards the body.

pinned to the floor and bring his elbow near to his body. Now raise his elbow towards the ceiling with your right arm. The lock will come on straight away at the shoulder; do not forget to keep the pressure on your partner s chest because if not he will have the chance to turn his body and escape.

The-Knee-on-the-Belly

The Americana is a submission that can be applied from the side mounted position. In contrast, the knee-on-the-belly is another powerful and dominant position that you can move into from the side mounted position.

Knee on the belly.

Grip the leg and collar.

The knee-on-the-belly position is extremely powerful and an effective one to move into if you are finding it difficult to find an opening from which to apply a submission technique while you are in the side mounted position. The knee-on-the-belly shows superiority and control over your opponent, and in competition you will be awarded two points if you can hold this position for 4sec. It is one that will put your opponent under enormous pressure, and, because your opponent will find this position uncomfortable, he will have to work hard to escape. Often when he is doing so he will give you the opportunity to submit him.

The Technique

Start by putting your partner in the side mounted position as before. When you grasp your partner s gi behind his head, grasp a little deeper and to the opposite side of his body. This will help you to keep control over your partner s head and prevent his turning. Your other hand is gripping your partner s trouser at knee level. Keep this grip strong. As you have seen earlier, one of your knees will be pushed tight against your partner s hips in the side mount. Take this knee and slide it up and on to his stomach. Your other leg needs to be stretched out behind you and slightly towards the side so that you have an excellent base. Bring your head up and drive your knee down into your partner s belly by pulling hard with both hands. If you can hold this position for 4sec you will get two points. It is when you have complete control from this position that you can move to other dominant ones, such as the mounted position, and keep accumulating points as you search for an opportunity to finish the fight with a submission.

The Arm Bar from the Knee-on-the-Belly Position

The arm bar is a simple and effective elbow lock. It is popular in Brazilian iu-jitsu because it works and can be applied from many positions. You will already be aware that the arm bar can be applied from the basic guard position, and we shall come back to it again when we look at other positions. What is important to remember is that the application of the arm bar is exactly the same from whatever position you apply the technique, but your position will determine how you try to start the technique and trap your opponent s arm. It is important to get these first moves in

Apply pressure down and pull.

Arm lock from knee on belly.

applying the technique right otherwise you will lose control of the technique and provide your opponent with the opportunity to escape. The arm bar is a natural technique to apply from the knee-on-the-belly position because your opponent will be desperate to escape from this position and, in most cases, will try to push you away. In trying to do this, your opponent will straighten and stretch his arm, the perfect invitation for you to apply the arm bar. Remember that if you are caught by your opponent with his knee on your belly do not try to push your opponent away and straighten your arm. This is quite simply the wrong way to escape. You have to keep your arms close to your body and protect yourself from the arm bar.

Grip the sleeve.

The Technique

You are in the knee-on-the-belly position with excellent control over your partner s body. You have a good grip with both hands, your head is well up, your base is good and your knee is driving downwards into your partner s stomach. Your partner

is uncomfortable, is trying to escape and stretches out his arm to push you away. With the arm that is holding your partner s trousers and controlling his hips, you hold his wrist and press the wrist and the arm tight to your chest. You move your left hand to the middle of your

Push down with free hand.

Pass the leg.

partner s chest and lean slightly forward so that all your weight is coming down through both your arm and knee on to his body. This downward pressure will stop your partner from being able to turn and therefore escape. You now use the leg that you have stretched out behind you to give you a good base and pass it over your partner s head and sit back on the floor. By sitting back you now have his arm trapped between your legs, and the leg nearer his head is across his chest. The closer your buttocks are to your partner s body, the better the technique and the less room he has to turn and try to escape. Try not have a gap between your legs, try and keep the arm as firmly between your legs as possible by pushing your knees together since you will make the finishing position really tight and this makes it hard for your partner to pull his arm back. Once you are in this position all that you need to do is to lie back and lift your hips up towards the ceiling. This will force the arm to straighten and, if you continue to straighten the arm, it will

Sit back.

overextend and fracture at the elbow. When you have the arm bar, make sure that the hand that is trapped against your chest has the thumb pointing up towards the ceiling since this will make sure that your partner s elbow is properly trapped against your hips.

Opposite side arm lock from knee on the belly.

Control the arm.

The Arm Bar from the Knee-on-the-Belly on the Opposite Side of Your Opponent

The arm bar can be applied from many positions, but it can also be applied in different ways from the same position. Here we are going to look at exactly the same position, the knee-on-the-belly, but also how to attack your opponent s arm in a completely different way, but with the same finishing technique, the arm bar. Remember that the application of the arm bar is exactly the same, but how you start the technique and trap your opponent s arm is different. Your opponent is desperate to escape from the knee-on-the-belly position but does not want to push you away and in doing so straighten his arm, because he knows that this is the perfect opportunity for you to apply the arm bar. Instead he is going to try and push your knee off his stomach, turn and thus escape.

Pass the leg to the other side.

The Technique

You have the knee-on-the-belly position and your partner tries to push your knee away from his stomach with his left arm and turn his hips to the side to escape. However, you can counter by putting your right hand inside his left arm. Keep your knee on his belly and put your left

Finish.

hand on the floor just outside his triceps. Both your hands are now on the opposite side of your opponent and this will make a good base for you to be able to turn to the other side, passing your left leg over his head. This will turn your body through 180 degrees so that you are now sitting on the opposite side of your partner s body, with your right leg over his chest and your buttocks tight to the side of his ribs. Make sure that you fit your left foot tightly under his left shoulder and that your legs are both tight against his arm. Now you need only to lie back and straighten your partner s arm. When you are passing to the other side, do not forget to use your left hand to grip and keep his arm tight to your chest. It is important to hold his arm correctly so that you get the technique right. During the pass to the other side, keep your hips and body low since this will deny your partner any space in which to turn and escape.

The North—South Position

This position is also known as the sixty-nine position in Brazilian jiu-jitsu. It is another good one from which to dominate and control your opponent. The reason for including it in this chapter is that it is a posi-tion that you can readily move into from the side mounted position, and this is particu-larly useful if you cannot stabilize that or gain the knee-on-the-belly position. The north—south position is such a dominant one since it gives you great control of your opponent s head, because your body is lying directly on top of his head, and this means that you are well away from his legs, making it difficult for him to escape and trap you in his guard.

The Technique

To stabilize this position you need to place your chest over your partner s head and push your legs out behind you. This means that the bulk of your weight is pushing down through your chest on to his head. This is important because, if he cannot turn his head, he has no chance of turning his body. Use both hands to make sure that you get a good grip of either side of your partner s gi from underneath his arms. This will put pressure on him and give you control of his shoulders as well as head. Remember that your body weight must be concentrated downwards on to his head in order to obtain a really good position.

The
north–south
position.

The Arm Bar from the North—South Position

After you have learnt and mastered the north—south position, you will be able to apply many different submissions from it. As you are at your opponents head, you will have a choice of which side you wish to attack from. This gives you a great advantage. Do not waste it by practising your finishing techniques from one side only. If you practise to the left and the right so that you are comfortable on both you will, quite simply, have doubled your opportunities to attack your opponent and win.

Arm lock from north–south.

The Technique

Get your partner in the north—south position and gain firm control of his head. Both arms are holding his gi lapel and controlling his arms and shoulders. Change your right-hand grip so that you are now gripping your own gi lapel. This simple change in grip gives you control over your partners right arm and this is the arm that you are going to attack. Make sure that you grip your own lapel on the left side of your gi and near to your neck; this will give you a tight grip on your partners arm. After that, move up and to the right side of him, passing your left leg over his head. You are now sitting next to your partner, with your buttocks tight to his ribs. Your left leg is across his head and your right leg is bent, with the foot pushed tight underneath his side. His arm is trapped against your chest and the elbow against your pelvis. You are now in the perfect position to execute the arm bar, lie back and push your hips up towards the ceiling and straighten your partners arm. Remember that the thumb of the hand that you have trapped against your body should be facing up towards the ceiling since this locks the elbow against your hips and makes it difficult for your opponent to escape.

Grab your lapel to control the arm.

Pass the leg.

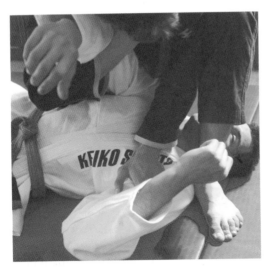

Control the shoulder.

Sit back.

Final Comments

Much of this book has been about getting you to flow from one position to another so that you can control your opponent s body and work an opening from which to finish him. This chapter has given you three different positions from which to control and dominate your opponent, but has applied the same finish from each position, the arm bar. This is not the only submission that you can apply from these positions but it is one of the most simple and effective. By describing this finish from three positions you can see how versatile this finishing technique can be and how imaginative you can and should be as a Brazilian jiu-jitsu fighter. A good fighter should be able to flow from one position to another, and a good training drill with your partner is to assume one of the positions described above and move from one to the other without trying to finish. This will make you much more comfortable about changing position and

Stretch the arm to finish.

keeping a good base all the time that you are moving around your partner s body. Your ability to do this and keep control of his balance is fundamental to your ability to work your opponent into a position from which you can finish.

8 The Mounted Position and Its Submissions

As you are well aware by now, Brazilian jiu-jitsu focuses primarily on fighting on the ground. A fighter does not want to fight his opponent standing up but to take the fight to the ground as quickly as possible. Brazilian jiu-jitsu was developed as a fighting art in the belief that most fighters learn and develop their skills in the stand-up position and neglect their skills on the ground. Brazilian jiu-jitsu fighters developed their art in the heat of competition, against fighters from many different styles of the martial arts. By taking their opponent to the floor these fighters took their opponents out of their comfort zone, out of the stand-up positions that they predominately trained in and put them under pressure in an environment that they were not used to, the floor. Boxing is a wonderfully effective fighting art in the stand-up position, but little that you learn in a boxing club will prepare you for the ground fighting techniques available to a Brazilian jiu-jitsu fighter. This style focuses on the weaknesses of the other martial arts. Brazilian jiu-jitsu does not claim to be any more effective in the stand-up position than any other martial art since it was designed for the floor.

The mounted position is the most valued position that you can attain in Brazilian jiu-jitsu. It is the position that a fighter will hunt for the most in competition, particularly if he is fighting an opponent from another martial art. This is the position that you want to gain most of all as a Brazilian jiu-jitsu fighter, because this is where you can put your opponent under the most pressure. In a Brazilian jiu-jitsu competition you will be awarded four points for achieving the mounted position. The pressure you can then put your opponent under is immense, and he will be quite desperate to escape, giving you plenty of opportunity to get a submission. You have an extensive range of chokes, strangles and locks that you can apply from this position. The mounted position has also proved to be one of real strength in the mixed martial arts arena and in vale tudo. Many think that Brazilian jiu-jitsu and valet tudo are the same thing, but this is not the case. Brazilian jiu-jitsu is primarily a grappling art, and you are not allowed to use punches, kicks, knee strikes or elbow strikes in a Brazilian jiu-jitsu competition. However, Brazilian jiu-jitsu has had a very strong influence on vale tudo and mixed martial arts competition, because Brazilian jiu-jitsu fighters have been able to dominate those from other disciplines on the floor. The mounted position has proved to be ruthlessly effective in Brazilian jiu-jitsu, vale tudo and mixed martial arts. If you gain the mounted position in a vale tudo or mixed martial arts fight not only can you use all the submissions techniques available in Brazilian jiu-jitsu, but you can also use all the punches and elbow strikes that are common to the other martial arts, making it almost impossible for your opponent to defend himself effectively. So many good fighters from other martial arts come to the Sleeping Storm Dojo and say to Ricardo, I do not feel that I am the complete fighter, I have excellent skills in the stand-up position, but I do not know enough about fighting on the floor to be really comfortable and effective. So it is for many martial artists all over the world, and this is why so many fighters have turned to Brazilian jiu-jitsu to give them that extra edge in vale tudo and mixed martial arts competition. The complete fighter must be able to fight standing up as well as on the floor, and the complete fighter will use the mounted position ruthlessly and effectively to win his fights.

The Mounted Position

The mounted position is not unique to Brazilian jiu-jitsu. You will also see it in judo, but no other martial art, including judo, has ever come close to developing this position with such effect. It is important, therefore, that you feel comfortable in this position and that you can spend time in it and put your opponent under constant pressure. This will happen only if you can get and maintain a good base. The description below will give you the technical knowledge to execute the position but only time on the mat and practice will develop your balance and understanding of it. I strongly recommend that when you practise with your partner you put him in the mounted position and that he tries to escape

without your trying to finish him. Only then will you start to develop the skill that you will need to keep your opponent in this position for long periods.

The Technique

Your partner is on his back and you sit on his chest. It is important that you sit on his chest and not his stomach. If you sit on his chest he will obviously find it difficult to breathe and you will put him under immense pressure to escape. You will also have control over his shoulders, making it impossible for him to sit up or turn and therefore escape. Drive your knees up tight into your partner s armpits. This gives you a better grip with your legs and drives his arms above his head. The arms are much weaker if they are above shoulder height, so this will limit what your partner can do with his arms. Keep your feet tucked in tight to your partner s sides. This will help you to drive your weight down through your hips on to his chest, making it difficult for him to turn and escape. It also means that if he arches his back in an attempt to throw you off you are glued to his chest, making it difficult to shift your weight and body from the centre of his chest.

The mount.

Submissions from the Mounted Position

Now that you have been introduced to the mounted position we are going to look at some of the submissions you can employ from it. Remember that you are in a very dominant position and it is your opponent who is under pressure. Do not panic and think that you have to apply a submission technique the moment you gain the mounted position. Too many fighters rush when they are in the mounted position, the adrenaline is pumping around and they quite naturally want to win the fight as quickly as possible, so they push too hard and make a mistake, giving their opponents the opportunity to escape. A good Brazilian jiu-jitsu fighter is patient and understands that in the mounted position it is he that is in control of the fight. You can afford to wait and use this position to make your opponent give you the opportunity to finish. Use this position wisely and take your time to exploit all the opportunities that will inevitably come your way.

The Arm Bar

We have covered this technique from a number of other positions and by now you should realize how devastatingly effective this technique is. When you watch a Brazilian jiu-jitsu class or competition you will see the arm bar done again and again. Every fighter will learn this move, but the fighters who execute this really well are those who pay attention to the little details. These fighters have excellent technical control and can apply the arm bar from many different positions; but they can also disguise their movements really well. Sometimes you will be unable to see or feel the fighter move into position for the arm bar and you will be aware that this is the

technique the fighter is going for only when he is in the final position and actually applying the technique. Disguise and the ability to change from one finishing technique to another from the same position are important in Brazilian jiu-jitsu. A common example of this from the mounted position occurs if you try to attack your opponent s neck with a choke or a strangle. Your opponent will try to defend his neck by blocking your attack with his arm; this will give you control of his arm and the perfect position from which to attack his arm with the arm bar. By initiating one attack from the mounted position, another opportunity has presented itself, so take it. The pressure you can exert from this position will create opportunities you may not have expected, be flexible and alert so that you can make the most of them.

The Technique

Get your partner into the mounted position and take hold of his right arm high up on the triceps with your right arm. Bring the arm in tight to your body with a good, strong grip, because you will hold the arm in this position to the end of the movement. Put your left hand firmly on your partner s left shoulder, with strong downward pressure to make sure that his back does not come off the mat. Move your body around to your left, trapping the arm to your body more tightly. In competition you can put your hand on your opponent s chin, but in practice put your hand on his shoulder. This will help you to stay friends with him! Lift your right leg and stretch your body forward; you must make sure that your partner s elbow is against your navel and that you apply continuous, downward pressure with your left hand on your partner s shoulder since this will help you to turn your body around his left arm. Put your body weight over your right leg and pass your left leg over your partner s head. You are now

Control the arm lock for the lock.

Put pressure on the shoulder.

Sit your weight on your arm and leg.

Pass the leg.

sitting next to him, with your buttocks tight against his ribs and with both your legs lying over his body. Simply sit back and stretch your body out towards the floor, keeping hold of your partner s arm. The pull on his right arm will straighten the arm and, when your back touches the floor, push your hips up towards the ceiling. This will force the arm to extend even further, bringing the lock on at the elbow. If you push too far and too hard you will fracture your partner s arm at the elbow joint. Make sure that the point of his elbow is facing down against your pelvis. You can achieve this by making sure that the

Stretch the arm to finish.

Sit back.

hand you have trapped against your chest has the thumb pointing up towards the ceiling. Always keep your legs pushing down on your partner s body, this will make sure that he cannot sit up nor turn, which would make it possible for him to escape.

The Arm Bar Variation

By now we know that we can apply the arm bar from many different positions, and, for me, this is what makes Brazilian jiu-jitsu so interesting. Just when you think you are safe and in a good position, your opponent will come back at you with a counterattack and apply a technique such as the arm bar from a position you have never seen before. The importance of vale tudo and mixed martial arts competitions in Brazilian jiu-jitsu has put the pressure on it to keep developing. In judo there is a strict syllabus of techniques that you must learn to obtain the successive belts and this has changed little over many years. By contrast, Brazilian jiu-jitsu is constantly evolving and changing, with fighters looking for new ways to apply

different techniques. As Brazilian jiu-jitsu has started to spread far from the shores of Brazil, so these variations in technique and the application of them have multiplied. Brazilian jiu-jitsu is an art that embraces technical change and development, making it a difficult one to define and counter in the arena. It is hoped this book will give you some idea of the different positions from which we can apply just this one technique, the arm bar, and therefore provide some idea of the technical brilliance and complexity of the art. If you are fighting someone who has more knowledge than you in a no-gi fight then the arm bar is a useful technique to try to apply. The arm bar is a submission technique that you should learn to use frequently in attack. If you are fighting a superior and more skilful opponent you will need to press for a quick submission. The arm bar is a technique that you are looking to apply as quickly as possible, because it is simple but effective. If your opponent is better than you, you will need to keep the fight simple and direct, rather than be drawn into a complex technical fight that plays to his strengths.

Mounted arm bar variation.

Control the arm and shoulder.

Turn your body.

Pass the shine over the neck.

The Technique

Get your partner in the mounted position with a good firm base so that he cannot reverse the position easily. He starts to push you away by putting his right hand on your chest in an attempt to escape from the position. You hold his right wrist with your left hand with a strong grip, maintaining it until you finish the move.

You must use your partner s movement as he is trying to push you away to make him go towards his left side. Then, standing on your right leg, turn your body to your left; you are going to pass your left knee over his head, bringing the knee tightly into his arm and letting your foot make a hook around his neck. You are then going to move towards the floor

Reverse view.

Roll forward the stretch the arm.

Reverse view.

Note the position of the foot.

by putting your left shoulder on the mat with your face towards your partner s feet. To keep this position as tight as possible, you must keep your body as close to your partner s body as you can, keeping the elbow in tight to your stomach or you will lose the position. You are now able to apply the arm bar: just stretch out your body and push your hips forward, forcing your partner s arm to straighten. Sometimes you can lose control of the arm that you trapped against your body and then you have to put your partner s arm back in place against your body to obtain the submission. Do not be afraid to readjust your position if you do not execute the move perfectly. Only practice will make perfect.

Choke from the mount.

Grip thumb out.

The Choke from the Mounted Position

Chokes and strangles play a central role in Brazilian jiu-jitsu so it is important that you learn how to choke your opponent into submission properly. Chokes are effective because they prevent your opponent from breathing and no one can continue to fight if he cannot gain his breath, no matter strong and powerful he is. As we have said before, Brazilian jiu-jitsu is a tactical game in which disguise and the ability to change from one finishing technique to another from the same position are important. Different fighters will have different strengths and weaknesses, some can defend their arms very well and therefore make it hard for you to submit them with arm locks, but in protecting their arms so effectively they may leave themselves vulnerable to attack from the choke or the strangle. This is what I like about Brazilian jiu-jitsu, it is like a game of chess — sometimes gu wait for your opponent to make a mistake, sometimes you go on the attack, sometimes you pretend to make a move for one technique but set yourself up to apply

another, and sometimes you pretend to make a mistake in order to get the chance to counter-attack. The choke that we are going to do now is simple and effective, but remember with this technique to use your body weight as this will help to make the choke strong and thus help you to control the position, as well giving you a much stronger base. This choke can be applied from either side so that you must practise both the left and the right.

The Technique
Get your partner in the mounted position with a good firm base to prevent him from escaping. Use your right hand to make a strong grip inside the lapel of his gi, at his left lapel. The palm of the hand should be flat against the inside of the gi and your thumb should be on the outside of the gi, making a deep and strong grab. Now with your left hand take a grip with your thumb inside. This should leave your arms crossed in front of your partner s throat. You then put your weight forward on to your arms and push your elbows out towards the side, thereby scissoring and drawing your arms tightly across your

Grip thumb in.

Squeeze the throat.

partner s neck. You can increase the pressure on the neck if you need to by pushing your weight forward until your head touches the mat just above his head. Be careful not to lose your base and thereby loosen the choke.

Final Comments

The mounted position is the one that you want to get to in a fight because this is where you can put your opponent under the most pressure. However, do not waste the mounted position by rushing in. You have an extensive range of chokes, strangles and locks that you can apply from the position, so take your time to get the right one. It is important therefore that you feel comfortable in the mounted position and that you can spend time in it. When you practise this position put your partner into it and see whether your partner can escape without your trying to finish him. This drill will be crucial to you in developing the skill that you will need to keep your opponent in this position for long periods. Disguise and the ability to change from one finishing technique to another from

Lean forward to tighten.

the same position are very important in Brazilian jiu-jitsu, and the mounted position is the perfect one from which to confuse or deceive an opponent. By initiating one attack from the mounted position you will often create the opportunity to finish your opponent with a different technique, so take it.

9   Getting to Your Opponent s Back

Much of this book has been about gaining a dominant position over your opponent and then finishing the fight. A Brazilian jiu-jitsu fighter will look to dominate his opponent from a number of different positions; the mount position, the side mounted position, the knee-on-the-belly and the opponent s back. This chapter will look at gaining the advantage by getting to your opponent s back, and then some of the submissions you can employ from there. Gaining control of your opponent from the back has some obvious advantages: first, he cannot see you and therefore it is difficult for him to predict your next move; secondly, your opponent s options are limited in this position, he cannot use his legs to sweep or trap in you into the guard and he will have only limited use of his arms, making it both difficult to attack you and to defend himself against your attacks. What is more, your opponent will find it difficult to defend his neck in this position. If you manage to gain the back position properly he will also find it difficult to counter and escape from it. You will therefore have the opportunity to take your time and develop your dominant position into a finish at your own pace. Brazilian jiu-jitsu is different from other martial arts because of the time you spend on the floor. This means that fighters have the time to exploit their opponent s weaknesses on the floor and this makes them dangerous because when they are on the floor they are entirely comfortable and can afford to be patient. Gaining the back position will give you the time to control your opponent on the floor, while you work an opening for a finish. This is particularly relevant in no-gi and mixed martial arts contests, where you cannot use your opponent s gi to control or finish him, and where your opponent may have superior stand-up fighting skills.

Getting and Keeping the Back Position

A simple and common way of gaining the back position begins when you are in the mounted position and your opponent is trying to escape. Very often your opponent will turn his body in an attempt to throw you off, but, if you keep your base and let him turn, you will stay on top and he will end by facing down, with you now on his back. This is probably the most common way to get to your opponent s back and gain the back position. When you are on top and your opponent is underneath, with your front to his back, this is the back position. When you have gained it, with your feet hooked inside your opponent s legs, you can grasp his lapels and roll on to your back, pulling him with you. This is a good position for you to be in because your opponent now has little contact with the floor, making it difficult for him to gain any kind of base and much easier for you to control his balance and therefore control his movements. It is, however, essential that when you are in the back position (underneath or on top), that you hook your feet into the front of your opponent s hips. If you do not do so you will not have the grip necessary to keep the back position and your opponent will be able to escape. However, when you do so do not be tempted to change your position and cross your legs in the

Taking the back.

Opponent tries to escape.

Takes the back.

Hooks in and in control from the top.

misguided belief that this will give you a better grip. If you cross your legs then your opponent will be able to apply a simple but effective ankle lock. Getting control of your opponent from the back is very effective, but it is only so if you get that control with your legs. If your feet are not locked into the front of his hips he will be able to turn himself in towards you and trap you in the guard. If you gain the back position with your feet hooked into the front of his hips he is in trouble, and you are in a really good position, because, if you maintain it, you have many techniques available to you with which to finish the fight. And even if you decide to go to another position you can keep control over your opponent and make sure that the new position you move to is still a dominant one. If you gain the back position it is vital that you get the hook in to your opponent s hips as quickly as possible so that you can maintain and exploit the opportunities of the position, whether you are on top or underneath.

93

Rear mount from the bottom.

Alternative position.

Submissions from the Back Position

Now let us look at exploiting this dominant position by using some possible finishes. There are now so many possible techniques that you can use to finish a fight that it would be pointless to try to cover them all. Therefore we shall cover three simple but effective ones. These will be the mata-le o , the choke with gi lapel and the arm bar. Practise these until you are comfortable

with them since they will make you a very effective fighter from the back position. However, do not limit yourself to just these three, be aware that, as you master the back positions and become more comfortable with them, other finishing opportunities will develop. Take advantage of them and develop your own style so that you are not a predictable fighter. Learn the basics well and do not try to run before you can walk, but the back positions will give you plenty of opportunity to look at a range of techniques with which to submit your opponent.

The Mata-le o

The mata-le o is a choke and common in Brazilian jiu-jitsu, no-gi fights and mixed martial arts contests. It is common because it is simple, devastatingly effective and a powerful submission; many fighters pass out in this position, this is usually because they think that they are strong and can resist the technique and, naturally, do not want to lose the fight. Most fighters will try and resist the technique by stiffening the body, but this will actually make the choke stronger and they will lose their breath quickly and pass out if they do not tap immediately. Be very careful and keep your attention on your opponent, do not hold this choke if he is passing out, it would be very dangerous for him. This choke is fast, simple and effective, so do not use strength but instead develop a good technique at your own pace.

The Technique

Start in the back position, but with you and your partner sitting on the mat. Make sure you have control of the position and your partner by hooking your heels into the front of his hips. It does not matter which arm you use to execute this choke. If you use the right one pass your right arm around your partner s neck and then place your right hand on your left biceps. Your left hand will then have to pass behind your partner s head, pushing it forward and

Mata-leão.

Hold the biceps.

Pass the hand behind the head.

Push the head forward and lean back.

putting pressure on the back of the neck. Your right arm is around your partner s neck. Now twist it so that the blade of the arm (the bone of your forearm) is tight against your partner s throat. Now sit back and stretch out straight, as if you were leaning back and thrusting your hips towards the ceiling. This powerful move-ment from your hips will put tremendous pres-sure on your partner s neck and finish him quickly. This is why it is so important that you have hooked your heels into the front of his hips because without the hook you would not be able to use the power from your hips to make this such an effective finish.

Choke from the Back Position by the Lapel

Again, this choke is common to both Brazilian jiu-jitsu and judo. It is useful because when you fight an experienced opponent he will expect you to attack him with the mata-le o if you have the back position. Your opponent will protect himself by crossing his arms over his neck to stop you from getting your arm around his neck and therefore making it impossible to execute the famous mata-le o. So this is another way to choke your opponent from the back position if you cannot get an opening for the mata-le o.

Gi choke from rear mount.

The Technique

Start this choke as if you were trying get the mata-le o, but you cannot pass your arm around your partner s neck so instead you get hold of the lapel of his gi. Make sure you have a good, strong grip. If you are using your left hand you must hold your partner s right lapel. You must then move your hips out towards the right side so that you can grip his right trouser leg at the side of the knee. Now, you take the right hook off and move your right leg over his hips, but being careful not to let the left hook off because, if you do, the move will lose power and the pressure will be reduced. Then you pull the lapel of the gi and the trouser leg at the same time. The gi will pull tight against the throat of your partner and choke him. It is important to know which way to put pressure on his neck. When you are using the lapel you must never pull just the lapel and rely on the strength of your wrist only. You should draw your hand around in a semi-circular move-ment and pull the trousers in the opposite direction with your other hand. Use your legs and the left hook in particular to pin your partner and prevent him from turning with the choke. This will allow you to increase the twist on his body and therefore increase the strength and effectiveness of the choke.

Grip the collar and knee.

Pass the legs.

Push and pull to finish.

The Arm Bar

We have covered the arm bar technique already and the reason for putting it in again is to emphasize how the same finishing technique can be applied from different positions. We have looked at the arm bar from the guard position, but this technique is not limited to that. As indicated before, the arm bar is an excellent technique because it is simple and can be applied from so many different positions. The application of the arm bar is the same no matter position you are in, but it will determine how you try to start the technique and trap your opponent s arm. It is essential to get these first moves right otherwise you will lose control of the technique and provide your opponent with the opportunity to escape. In most cases you will get the chance to apply the arm bar whenever your opponent begins to straighten his arm. However, the back position gives you the opportunity to gain control of the arm and to apply the arm bar when your opponent s arm is bent.

The Technique

Start in the back position but with you and your partner sitting on the mat. Make sure you have control of the position and of your partner by hooking your heels into the front of his hips. To prevent you from getting the mata-le o y our partner has crossed his arms and covered his neck. This protects his neck, but it tends to leave his elbows out at his side. The space left between his arm and his side is the one you want to exploit to your advantage. Slip your left arm through this space, underneath his elbow and grip his wrist, giving you control of the arm. Break the hook you have on your partner s left hip, twist your body to the left and snake your left leg across the front of his hips. Pull him back

97

Arm lock from rear mount.

Pass the arm inside your opponent's arm.

towards the mat and break the right hook on his hips. As your partner falls back towards the mat, use your right hand to push his head away to make room and bring your right leg over his head. You now have the arm bar position, with the arm of your opponent trapped against your torso and your legs pushing against his chest, and you are forcing his arm to straighten. Be careful and remember that your partner will tap if he is in trouble.

Final Comments

The back position is a dominant one and a vulnerable one for your opponent. It is a position that all Brazilian jiu-jitsu fighters will look to gain and keep and one that you should take the time to practise and work at because it will provide you with the platform to win many fights. Gaining

and keeping the hook on the front of your partner s hips is essential if you are going to develop the true potential of this position. A good practice drill for this position is to get the back position on your partner with the hook and then let him try to escape, without your going for any finishing techniques. This helps you to develop the skills you will need to keep this position in the heat of competition. As you get better then make it more difficult and get the back position, but without the hook. Your partner will then try to escape and you will try to get the hook with both feet and keep the back position. This will help to develop your skills at getting the hook on as quickly as possible when the opportunity for the back position arises in a fight. Try and develop the three finishes that we have described — the mta-le o , the choke with

Pass the legs and push the head.

Pull the arm.

Stretch to finish.

gi lapel and the arm bar — so tha you can execute them smoothly and quickly. As always, take your time, so that you develop good technique. If you need to use strength, then you are not technically correct. However, as I said earlier, do not limit yourself to just these three techniques, be aware that, as you master the back positions and become more comfortable with them, other finishing opportunities will develop. Learn the back positions well and these will give you plenty of opportunity to submit your opponent with a range of submissions.

10 Sweeps

A crucial theme in Brazilian jiu-jitsu is that of constantly fighting for a better position from which to attack. Attaining a better position from which to strike or move freely into a submission hold is at the core of all ground fighting. To attain a better position a fighter must achieve two goals: move himself into a better position, and move his opponent into an inferior one. The sweep is therefore a crucial skill, because it allows a fighter to move his opponent into an inferior position with the minimum of effort. Performed with a good technique, the sweep will also use an opponent s momentum to help to move the fighter into the better position from which the fight can be finished. The point has been made here several times as it is so important to Brazilian jiu-jitsu that a good fighter must have excellent positional skills, as well as excellent submission skills. There is no point in having good submission skills if you can never get into position to use them. Sweeps are important because these skills are a vital part of gaining a good position over your opponent.

A technically good Brazilian jiu-jitsu fighter does not need to use strength to apply a sweep. Instead he will use good technique. If you have to use strength, then you have not got the control over your opponent s body that you should have and you will need to go back and look at your technique again and improve. It is difficult to sweep an opponent who has a good base and you are certainly not going to be able to sweep a good fighter by strength alone, if his base is good. If you try to use just strength against an opponent with a good base then it is likely to be you who sacrifices your base and it will be your opponent who sweeps you for a better position. Obviously, power and strength are useful, but never without good technique. Strength can be of use in competition if your opponent has the same level of technical ability as you. If the fight is close then your superior fitness might just give you that edge that you need to win. However, nine times out of ten superior technique will overcome superior strength. The perfect combination is good technique aided by good conditioning and strength.

In Brazilian jiu-jitsu there are many different sweeps. There are different sweeps from the many positions you could be in, such as the basic guard, the half guard, the butterfly guard and the spider guard. Some sweeps will give you a better position and others will give you submissions such as the arm bar, strangles, leg-locks or chokes. If you watch fights between good fighters it is rare to see many submissions. Such fighters have sound defences and will give an opponent few chances to finish. Instead, at this level, most fights are won on points and the margin of victory is usually small, just one or two points. Your ability to sweep and gain a better position may just be the scoring move that wins you a close fight and be the difference between winning and losing.

This is also why maintaining a good base in Brazilian jiu-jitsu is so crucial because you are going to be difficult to sweep if you have one. The only way to stop your opponent from sweeping you is to gain and maintain a good base at all times. This is a vital part of your defence against sweeps and an opponent who is trying to passing your guard, as we saw in Chapter 6. Do not think that you always have to finish and submit your partner during practice. This can be counter-productive, especially if your partner is less skilled than you and therefore relatively easy to finish. One of the best drills you can do in Brazilian jiu-jitsu is to fight but with no finishing techniques so that you and your partner are constantly fighting and striving for better positions from which to control one another. This will develop your ability to flow from one position to another, constantly trying to keep control of your partner s body. It is drills such as these that will make you a good positional fighter and really develop your ability to sweep.

The Hugging Sweep

This is a sweep that you are going to apply when you have your opponent caught in your basic guard, with the guard closed. It is a good movement for beginners to learn because the move is a relatively simple one and you will able to apply it without too much difficulty. Another advantage in learning this sweep early on is that you have to really move your hips to do the sweep properly, and this will help you to get into good habits early. Learning how to move your hips properly is a crucial skill in Brazilian jiu-jitsu and in most teaching classes there will be drills to reinforce this and get you to move your hips correctly. This sweep should also be

one of the first that you learn because it is from the closed guard, and this is one of the first positions that you will learn when you start Brazilian jiu-jitsu. This basic guard position gives you good control over your opponent, and without such control of your opponent s body and base you will be unable to sweep.

For this particular sweep you will grip an opponent s arm and leg and then have a closed guard. However, when you have learned rather more, you must try to alter the move and not just rely on the basic closed guard. As you progress it is important to try this sweep with your guard open. Of course, it is important to keep a strong guard, but you must also develop your skills as a fighter and your ability to manipulate and play with your opponent with your guard open. A good fighter needs to create openings for himself and to put pressure on his opponent, and, if you can control your opponent from the open guard, it will give you more space and opportunity to apply sweeps and submissions.

The Technique
With your partner in your closed basic guard, you take hold of his right arm with your right, as if you were going to apply the arm bar, but, instead, you are going to pull his arm towards the floor, putting his elbow close to it by your right side. Now pass your left arm around your partner s back and hold his gi underneath the arm. Grip the gi on your partner s left side. Now you must pull his body towards you and put pressure on him by not letting him pull his arm back. You then move your head towards your partner s left side. To do this and get the correct position you have to use your hips to really move the whole of your body to your left. As soon as you have done this, you must get hold of your partner s left leg on the inside, but

Sweep from the guard.

Control the arm and hold the back.

Control the leg.

Move the hips.

you must always keep your arm bent. To prevent him from going for a submission you must now open your guard. You should also open your guard when you have this position because you must use your legs to help you to sweep your partner. You will now use your right leg to

push his hips away and pull on the leg you are holding with your left arm towards your shoulder, this will give you your partner s base. You now use one flowing movement to sweep your partner and turn him over on to his back. This turning movement will pull you around so that you

Sweep.

Reverse view.

finish in the mounted position. Pay attention and make sure that your foot does not become trapped below your partner s back, because, if your foot is caught, you will not be able to get a good base in the mounted position.

The Arm Bar Sweep

If you execute this sweep correctly you will finish it with an arm bar and therefore a submission position on your opponent. This is a simple but effective sweep, but the success of it will again depend on how you use your hips. To perform this sweep well you need to develop the ability to move your hips from side to side, and, if you practise this sweep on both sides of your partner, this will help you to develop the proper hip movement. You can start by practising the arm bar submission from the basic guard position and then move into the sweep. This will help you to develop both the correct hip movement and, importantly, disguise. Your opponent will not be able to read your next move

clearly since you could be going straight for the arm bar or the sweep. This will make it much more difficult for your opponent to defend against you because he will be uncertain which move you are going for. Keep on practising as much as you can so that you can execute the move smoothly and quickly.

The Technique

You are going to start this sweep with your partner in your basic guard, with the guard closed. Get a grip on his left sleeve with your right hand, but do not put too much pressure on the arm because you will have to perform this movement quickly. If you let your partner know that you are going to do the sweep then he will pull his arm back and make it much harder for you to do it. Now you have to hold your partner s right leg on the inside. To do this, you will have to open your guard and move to the side, as if you were going to go for the arm bar. At the same time, you are going to pass your left leg behind his right arm, putting pressure

Sweep to arm lock.

Control the arm and leg.

Open the guard and turn hips.

Sweep.

under the armpit. As you pull your partner s weight on to your left leg, push hard with this leg against his shoulder under the arm, pulling his left arm. This will make your partner spin and fall with his back on the floor. Remember that you should not pass your right leg underneath you opponent, unlike the previous sweep, but keep it free to pass over his head to get the arm Bar. When you have got the sweep you need to sit up with your buttocks tight to your partner s ribs. Now you are in the correct position from which to apply the arm bar.

Stretch to finish.

The Butterfly Guard Sweep

This is not generally used by beginners because it takes some time to develop the skills necessary to be properly comfortable in this position. However, it is one that is well worth working at and, once you have been training in Brazilian jiu-jitsu for a while and are comfortable with most of the basics, you should start to practise it. The butterfly guard is a powerful one if you know how to use it. Use it properly and you can work with much more space and therefore create many more opportunities from which to sweep your opponent. To develop your ability and skill in the guard position you will need to go to Chapter 4. However, to recapitulate briefly on the butterfly guard position: you are seated on the floor in front of your opponent; he will be kneeling, trying to pass your guard by either holding your trousers at the ankles on both sides or trying to get control by putting your feet together. Then you will move your body forwards, putting your

feet between his knees and pressing one foot to the inside of each knee, this will help you to keep your position. This is the basic butterfly guard, but this can be altered if you need more or less space, depending on which sweep you are going to employ.

The Technique
Sit in the butterfly guard, controlling your partner s right arm by holding it tight to your side. Your left arm will reach below his right arm and get a firm grip of his back. This position will hold him tightly to you. It vital that you have complete control since you need to have your body held as tightly and compactly as possible to your opponent. When this is achieved,

Sweep from the butterfly guard.

105

Sweep from the butterfly guard.

Hold the arm and back.

Sit back and pull.

Hook the leg.

rock backwards, pulling his weight on top of you so that he no longer has any base. You are then going to turn him to the side of the arm that you are controlling. If you have his left arm trapped, you are going to use your right leg and hook the outside of his left leg. This will prevent him from putting it on the floor to prevent your sweep. Then, using your inside hook on his right leg, you are going to sweep your partner to your right and into the mounted position.

Turn.

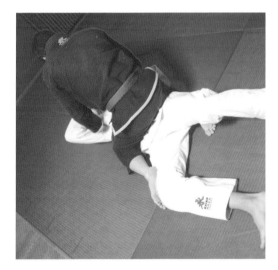

Finish in the mount.

Grabbing Both Ankles

This sweep, common in Brazilian jiu-jitsu, mixed martial arts and vale-tudo, is executed by grabbing both of your opponent s ankles. It is a sweep that you can employ when your opponent is trying to open your guard by standing up with a weak base. Executed correctly, it will give you a finishing position from which you can apply different leg and foot locks. Always be aware of your opponent s weaknesses. This particular sweep will be useful against an opponent who is uncomfortable in the stand-up position and is having problems in breaking your guard. Often when an opponent is having difficulty in opening your guard he will move to the stand-up position to break the guard as a last resort. He will be pushing hard to break the guard, and probably trying to use strength rather than technique. In this case your opponent will sacrifice his base and provide you with the perfect opportunity to execute the sweep.

The Technique

Put your partner in the basic guard, but this time, instead of kneeling down, he is standing up. You then use both hands to grab his ankles. The next step is to open your guard and lower your hips so that the back of your knees are resting against the front of your partner s knees. Then pull hard on his ankles, pulling his feet towards you, but at the same time use your legs to push his knees backwards. This will take his and force him to fall backwards to the floor. As your partner falls, follow him and use his momentum to help you to come up into the mounted position. This move is simple, but you will have to practise it carefully to get the sweep smooth and effective. Be careful with your partner s knees because, when you do this sweep, you are using your legs to push back against the front of his knees. This will force the knees back in the opposite direction to which they usually bend, causing them to hyperextend. So go softly and be careful not to injure your partner.

Sweeping a standing opponent from the guard.

Hold the ankles.

Push the knees.

Sweep.

Sit forward to
take the mount.

Final Comments

If you can sweep well you are always going to put your opponent under pressure and find better positions from which to attack. Attaining a better position from which to submit or control your opponent is fundamentally what Brazilian jiu-jitsu is all about. You will also make him unsure of his position because you will be able to attack his base. A good base is at the core of any good and effective technique, be it positional or submission. If a fighter does not have a good base then he will be unable to execute his techniques correctly. If you can relentlessly attack your opponents base then you are going to make it difficult for him to fight effectively and gain any kind of control of the fight. The sweep is therefore a crucial skill and one you should work hard to develop. To do this you will want to try them as often as you can in training. Try to fight only with an open guard. This will constantly give your partner the opportunity to pass your guard and you the opportunity to try to counter him with a sweep. To begin with, your partner is going to put you under real pressure and, more often than not, pass your guard, but this is training and not competition and we learn from our mistakes. By putting yourself under such pressure in training you are going to develop the very skills that are going to win your fights in competition.

11 Escapes

In this chapter we are going to assume the worse — that your fight has not gone according to plan, that you have come up against an opponent who is your equal and he has put you in real trouble. The truth is all fighters, however good they are, will find themselves in trouble at some point. We all make mistakes, particularly in competition, when the pressure is intense and the tendency is to rush and push for a finish as quickly as possible. It therefore makes sense to learn ways to escape from and to counter your opponents position. Many fighters get into trouble and are unable to escape because they do not include escapes in their daily training. Instead, these fighters concentrate on submission and positional techniques and forget to practise their escapes.

But how do you practise escape techniques? First of all, in Brazilian jiu-jitsu, as in any other sport, you need to have some humility and not be too self-important to be submitted by your partners. Of course, nobody wants to be submitted, but you must put yourself in difficult situations to develop the skills necessary in order to cope with them. If you are fighting with a partner who is less skilled than you what is the point of just submitting him whenever you want? In such a situation you are going to learn nothing new and gain little practice with the skills you already know. Instead, use this situation to develop your knowledge and put yourself under pressure. You will learn more if you fight lighter and try not to finish your partner but instead give the dominant positions to him. He can practise trying to pass your guard or developing a good

dominant position, and you can practise your sweeps or an escape to the side that you have the most difficulty with. This is the best way to train for escapes. If you do not put yourself in a dangerous position and never train in dangerous positions you will never have the skill or confidence to cope with them. To be a good and complete Brazilian jiu-jitsu fighter you must explore these escapes because you are going to need these skills in a competitive situation, and you will be unable to execute them properly unless you know how to escape with confidence, skill and speed. Normally, smaller men will assimilate the escape techniques quickly because they lack the strength to cover up their mistakes against bigger opponents in training. So they will have had to cope with difficult situations on a more regular basis in training when they first started Brazilian jiu-jitsu classes. However, because they have had to develop good technique from the outset and are more habituated to dealing with difficult positions in training, it is often the smaller student who will eventually develop into the better fighter than his bigger, stronger classmate. Remember: good technique will always overcome brute strength and aggression.

Escape from the Arm Bar

As you will be aware from the number of times that we have covered it, the arm bar is one of the most common submission techniques a Brazilian jiu-jitsu fighter will seek to employ. So an escape from the

Arm lock
escape.

arm bar submission is an important and useful skill to have, because your opponent will be seeking to apply this technique on you at any opportunity. The arm bar is an effective technique and you need to be careful when using it. If you do not tap at the right moment and your opponent keeps extending your arm then you will end with a broken arm. You need to balance bravery and skill with common sense. If you are going to use this escape and make it work you need to know what you are doing and have practised it in training so that you are confident and quick. This escape has to be done with speed and precision or it will not be worth it. You will get caught with the arm bar or give your opponent the opportunity to apply another submission, such as the omoplata or the triangle. A good tip is that the more your opponent straightens your arm, the more difficult it is going to be for you to escape. If your arm is nearly fully extended, tap and stay fit to fight another day.

The Technique
You will start the escape with your partner in the perfect position to apply the arm bar. However, you are defending one arm with your other by clasping your hands together. This will make it much too difficult for your partner to straighten your arm. In the first picture you can see that he is in the perfect position to apply the arm bar. You need to change this by moving your hips to your left. Now you have enough space to turn your body to the left and to stretch out your trapped arm. Your other arm must be straightened at the same time and then be passed underneath your body. By doing this and straightening your other arm you will be able to twist your body. When you have

111

Pass the arm under.

Turn.

Pass.

Side control.

twisted your body around, you must keep your head as close as possible to the outside of your partner s right leg since this will put pressure on the leg and prevent him from catching you in the triangle. Then, with your left hand, you need to catch hold of his gi behind his neck as quickly as possible. This will help you to gain the side mounted position and prevent him from attempting a counterattack. Now you have escaped from your partner s attempted arm bar and put yourself in the dominant side mounted position.

Escape from the Triangle

Another common submission in Brazilian jiu-jitsu is the triangle. Again, this is a powerful submission and, if your opponent manages to apply this technique properly, you will not have time to execute the escape because the pressure on your neck will be too great and you will pass out. As with the arm bar, you have to use common sense to know when to try the escape. If your opponent has not managed to execute the technique perfectly and has not got his legs into the right position you will be able to escape, but if the triangle is applied tightly and you cannot get into the right position to escape do not try to achieve the impossible but rather tap.

Escape from the triangle.

The Technique

Your partner has you in the triangle. Your first step is to use the arm trapped between your partner's legs to get hold of his trousers to your left side since this will take some of the pressure off your neck. Remember, if you leave your trapped arm out straight your partner will be able to get the arm bar on you. You have to make a strong grip on the trouser leg and push his leg to the side with your right arm. You have to use your arm to get some space because the triangle is a tight position and the only way you are going to be able to breathe is by pushing your partner's leg to the side and relieving some of the pressure on your neck. To keep this gap you must to put your chin close to your chest. Now you have to hold your partner's left lapel with your left hand to allow control, then stand up and pass your left leg over his head. Remember: if your partner gets hold of your leg he will have a chance to sweep you or, even worse, tighten the position. Next you have to lie down, stretching out and twisting your body

Hold the leg and lapel.

113

Stand and pass the leg.

Sit back.

Pull free of the choke.

around towards the side of your partner s body. This will pull your head out of the triangle and, while not leaving you in a particularly advantageous position, will allow you to escape without being choked.

The Arm Bar Escape from the Guard Position

This escape is relatively simple and all the more effective because you can employ it quickly. The secret to having good escape skills is to react to your opponent s move as early as possible. The later you try to counter the move, the more likely it is that he has a strong position. The sooner you can counter an attempt to apply the arm bar against you the less extended your arm will be, and the more space and time you will have in which to escape. However, the straighter your arm is, and therefore the later you try to escape from the arm bar, the less likely you are to succeed, because your opponent has a much greater control over your arm. The appeal of this particular escape is that you can use it whether your opponent is wearing a gi or not. You will also now be aware how important the guard position is in Brazilian jiu-jitsu; escapes from the guard position and the submissions that can be applied from it are also both important and useful. Remember: if you are caught in the guard or the triangle do not straighten your arms. This is an invitation to your opponent to try and submit you with the arm bar, and you would be making an already difficult situation even worse. Keep your arms protected all the time when you are in the guard by keeping them bent.

The Technique

Your partner has you in the guard, has control of your arm and is trying to apply the arm bar. As before, you must protect the arm that is being attacked by using your other arm. Hold the biceps of your free arm so that your two arms are linked and it is therefore more difficult for your partner to straighten the arm he is attacking, in this case the left. You then have to apply the maximum downward pressure that you can on your partner. This will prevent him from using his legs to stretch and straighten your arm for the arm bar. To get this pressure, move your knees off the floor and push your legs backwards, so that all your weight is being driven down through your partner, curling him back into a ball. However, make sure that your partner does not turn his body and get hold of one of your legs since he will then be able to sweep you. By putting such pressure on to him he cannot apply the arm bar because he cannot get the leverage with his legs to straighten your arm. Break your arm free from his grip so

Escape from the arm lock.

Protect the arm and pressure down.

Pull arm free.

Use the freed arm to control the collar.

Pass the guard.

that the arm is safe and then you can attempt to pass his guard by using your now freed arm to catch his lapel; continue to apply pressure on the legs and pass around, finishing in the side mount. When you learn any escape you must learn how to keep a good base all the time.

Upa — from the Mounted Position

As you are already aware from Chapter 8, the mounted position is the one that all Brazilian jiu-jitsu fighters hunt for and prize the most. If your opponent catches you in the mounted position you are in trouble and you will need to escape as quickly as possible, because the longer you spend in this position the more opportunity your opponent is going to have to finish you. This is an important escape to learn because the mounted position is such a fundamental part of Brazilian jiu-jitsu. To develop this escape properly you must practise hard; the mounted position is a dominant one and it will not be easy to escape. Your opponent is going to defend his position and make it as hard for you as possible. You will need to practise this escape on both the left and the right side because you are going to have to work hard for the smallest of opportunities to escape from the mounted position and you need to be able to take advantage of that opportunity as soon as it arises, whether it be on the left or the right. To practise this escape work with your partner rather than get into a full-on fight before either of you really knows what he is doing. Co-operate with one another, let your partner gain the mounted position and a good base, and then start practising the escape lightly. Just as when you started to learn other techniques, you and your partner should not apply too much pressure to begin with, but just enough to execute the escape correctly. Work on getting the technique better and then you and your partner can apply more power and speed gradually. This specific training will develop the skills you will need for this escape, so keep practising at a controlled speed until you can execute the move with complete control at full speed. Remember: when your opponent traps you in the mounted position you must always protect your neck and arms. Keep your arms bent and never try to push your opponent away and stretch your arm since this will give him the opportunity to submit you with an arm bar.

The Upa.

The Technique

Your partner has you in the mounted position, so you need to escape from this position as quickly as possible. Remember that your opponent will be awarded four points for gaining the position, but only if he has stabilized it. If you can escape from the position as soon as your opponent has achieved it he will not get the points for it because it was not stabilized. However, if it is not possible to escape immediately, take care to protect your arms and neck because your opponent will be looking to attack you. With the mounted position stabilized by your opponent you have to do the upa. This is a move used in different situations and is the Brazilian term for pushing your opponent up by bridging your body. To do this you need to first control one arm by pulling it across the body,

Hold the arm and back.

thereby preventing your partner from using it to prevent the move. Then reach your left arm behind your partner and grab his gi firmly and afterwards hook your left foot over his right foot, preventing him from using that leg to stop you. Then arch your body off the ground by lifting your hips as high as possible; this will bring your

Hook the foot.

Bridge and turn.

partner s weight forward. At the same time push him and yourself on to your left shoulder (since you have trapped his right arm and leg he should not be able to prevent you executing the move). This will twist your partner around so that he ends with his back on the floor and you on the top, but in his basic guard. Remember that you have to do this escape in one smooth movement, from the moment you have done the upa until you have completed the escape. This is a move that needs to be executed quickly and smoothly. Start practising with people who are of the same weight as yourself then, as you develop your skills, practise on others who are much heavier since this will make the move more difficult. This will be good preparation for competition when you fight people of similar weight to yourself.

Finish in the guard.

When Your Opponent Has the Back Position

As with all the other positions that we have looked at in this chapter, you do not want to get yourself into this position in competition. I personally fear my opponent gaining the back position as much as when he gains the mounted position, because both are ones of power and dominance for your opponent. Your opponent will gain four points for the back position and have the opportunity to go for a range of chokes, strangles and locks. As you will know by now, the back position is well known in Brazilian jiu-jitsu, mixed martial arts and vale-tudo. The position is a strong one whether you are fighting with or without a gi. In it your neck is vulnerable and your opponent will certainly be trying to apply the mata-le o, so the first rule is try not to get in to this position at all in competition. However, in training you must practise the escape from this position and give your partner the opportunity to finish you from it. Again, a useful drill for you and your partner is for him to try and stay in the back position without finishing you while you try and escape and seek a more dominant position. If you escape, then go back to your original position with your partner in the back position and do it all over again. You should repeat so that you become confident in what you are doing and in the escape. The other bonus is that your partner develops his positional skills from the back position. Then, when you are getting tired and thinking of stopping you should change over and do the same thing again, with you in the back position and your partner practising the escape. This is the way most Brazilian jiu-jitsu fighters train, with commitment and respect for their partners, because without good partners you are not going to improve.

The Technique

When you have your partner on your back turn him and put him flat on to his back. When you are on the top always push back on your partner s chest, using all your weight to pin him to the floor, but always protecting your neck to prevent him from submitting you with a choke or a strangle. With your right arm you are going to hold your partner s right leg, but keep your left arm up protecting your neck. When you have done that you are going to stretch your right leg out straight and push your partner s right leg away and thereby remove the hook that he has on the front of your hips with his right foot. Not having the hook on your right hip any longer means that you can now move

Escape from the rear mount.

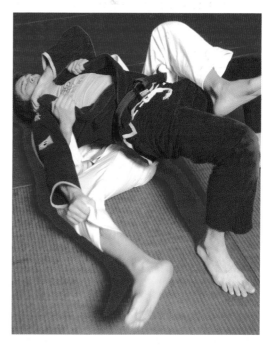

Move the leg.

119

Pass the leg.

Move the hips.

Finish in
side control.

your hips to the right until you can touch the floor with your buttocks. Do this by passing your right leg over your partner s right leg. With your left arm — that was protecting your neck — you are going to pass it under your partner s head, but always keep your weight pushing down on his chest. The position is now almost complete, but you will be stuck in the half guard if you do not continue the move. So, with your right hand, push down on your partner s left leg and pull your left leg out. When you have your leg free, change your base immediately so that you can get into the side mounted position and stabilize the position. Remember: always practise this particular escape on both the right and the left side and use control. Start slowly and gradually speed up as you get technically better. Do not sacrifice good technique for speed or strength.

Final Comments

For obvious reasons, the escapes that we have included in this chapter are the ones you would try if you were caught in some of the most common holds and locks. Those that we have looked at are the ones that your opponent is most likely to try because they are some of the most frequently met. But there are many locks and holds in Brazilian jiu-jitsu, and, since each is unique, so are the counters and the escapes. Brazilian jiu-jitsu is tactical, and for every attack there is a counter and an escape. You will never learn every attacking technique and you will never learn every counter or escape, but your knowledge and skill will develop the longer you train and the more you fight. For myself, I find it useful to ask my partner what I could have done to escape if he had managed to catch me with a technique I had never seen before. Rather than just accept that my partner is simply better than I, I want to take the opportunity of fighting someone more skilled to learn from. Most martial artists, and certainly most Brazilian jiu-jitsu fighters, are only too pleased to share their knowledge with you; so, if you do not ask, how are they to know what it is you wish to learn? Be positive in your attitude, training and desire to learn and you will become a much more rounded and accomplished fighter.

12 Eat Like a Brazilian Jiu-Jitsu Fighter

Good nutrition is a fundamental part of staying healthy and fit, whether you take part in a sport or not. Brazilian jiu-jitsu is like most other competitive contact sports in that any serious participant needs to pay attention to both conditioning and diet to be effective and to stay injury-free. Competitive fighters are categorized by weight, as in boxing or judo, so that fighters will compete against those of a similar stature. This means that most fighters do not want to develop the muscled physique of a weightlifter or a Rugby player. They want to be able to flow with their techniques rather than become stiff and rely on brute strength. This means that it is important for a fighter to maintain a lean physique, with excellent muscle tone. The fighter wants to maximize his power to weight ratio, to be able to generate power with good stamina and flexibility. The demands of Brazilian jiu-jitsu on the body are such that any regular participant needs to develop a good general level of fitness. You need to be strong, with excellent endurance and good flexibility. A proper, sensible, well-balanced diet is fundamental in achieving this aim. In writing this chapter I have highlighted sound dietary habits that are the basis for anyone who wants to be healthy and active. What I have tried to do is explain why and how these principles are used in Brazilian jiu-jitsu to improve a fighter s performance and training. Eat properly and you will enjoy your sport more and be more effective.

Another important reason for including a chapter on diet is that in Brazil access to clean water and good quality food is not always available. As in other countries, some of the best fighters come from the poorest and most deprived backgrounds. It is only by being successful that some can afford to get the proper nutrition they require to develop and stay at the top of their game. In a country with such a huge population the competition is fierce and always improving and developing. Diet and fitness training are something all Brazilian jiu-jitsu fighters and schools take, seriously.

Where Do I Start?

Any proper and sensible diet must include a wide variety of natural, unprocessed foods from all the food groups. These include carbohydrates (including vegetables, whole grains and fruit), protein and fats. By having variety you increase the likelihood of including all the nutrients, vitamins and minerals that are required for a healthy, balanced diet. A variety of foods also ensures that the diet remains interesting.

Water

Adequate hydration is a crucial part of health and a fundamental part of sports performance. Even a small water loss can impair both mental and physical functions, something a fighter cannot afford to have happen. The average adult requires at least 2 to 3ltr of water a day, and this requirement increases if you exercise. With Brazilian jiu-jitsu the fighter often wears a heavy grappling gi and the action is unrelenting. Thirst is a poor measure of dehydration because you become dehydrated long before you feel thirsty and so drink water continuously throughout the day. This is important during a competition or long training session when it is easy to forget to drink enough. Being well hydrated improves how you feel and perform. Alternatively, you can choose fruit teas, herbal blends and water flavoured with a little fresh fruit juice. The best measure of fluid balance is urine colour; this should be clear and pale at all times. Dark yellow urine is an indicator of dehydration.

Unfortunately, because Brazilian jiu-jitsu fighters compete in weight divisions, there is a strong temptation for them to lose weight by sweating unwanted weight off in the sauna or with a diuretic so that they can make a lower weight division. But to do so is to put their health seriously at risk and will almost certainly impair performance. A good example is from boxing, when Barry McGuigan lost his world title in the searing heat of the Nevada desert. By his own admission, a lack of attention to his drinking water between rounds destroyed his ability to beat his opponent.

Some useful tips to staying hydrated and healthy are:

¥   always have water available;
¥   start the day with a mug of freshly boiled water and a slice of lemon; in the summer add a sprig of mint and lemon slices to a jug of cold water;
¥   drink from a bottle of water to measure your daily intake until you are used to drinking enough;
¥   weigh yourself before and after exercise; for every kilogram lost, a litre of water is lost.

Good and Bad Fats

Contrary to popular thinking, not all fats are bad, many are good and a zero- or low-fat diet is harmful to your health in the long term. Saturated animal fats can increase the risk of heart disease, some cancers and strokes. These are generally solid at room temperature and found in meat and dairy products. Other good fats (containing the omega-3 and omega-6 essential fatty acids) play important roles in many functions of the body promoting health and well-being. Fats maintain skin and hair; they store and transport the fat-soluble vitamins A, D, E and K, they protect cell walls, control inflammation and support the immune system. The body cannot manufacture these essential fats so we need to obtain them from food. Omega-3 fatty acids are found in oily fish, such as salmon, trout, sardines, mackerel, herring and tuna; such fish should be included in the diet at least four times a week. Any serious participant in Brazilian jiu-jitsu will regularly expend a large amount of energy in training and it is vital to rest properly in order to recover thoroughly from training and competition. Good fats play a vital role in the fighter s ability to recover and train because they are a vital source of nutrients needed for repair and the maintenance of healthy tissue. The processes of repair and recovery are important because they allow the fighter to sustain his training over long periods, which is so necessary in order to develop. However, these good fats also aid the short-term recovery, a precious component of a fighter s make-up if he is going to have several fights in one day and progress through the rounds necessary to win competitions.

Carbohydrates

It is likely that half the amount of energy in your diet will come from carbohydrates. Those that are absorbed from the stomach rapidly cause blood glucose levels to rise (these carbohydrates are usually sweet-tasting, highly refined sugars, as in biscuits). This rise in blood glucose results in large amounts of insulin being released into the blood, and this means that blood glucose levels drop very quickly. As glucose levels are driven down by insulin, energy levels will drop and this results in hunger just a few hours after eating. The glucose removed from the blood by the insulin is often stored in the tissues as fat, so that this extra drive on appetite increases the tendency for long-term weight gain. For any athlete a constant, steady release of energy is imperative for effective performance. This is particularly true for Brazilian jiu-jitsu when fights may go on for a long time and the fighter may have to compete in several rounds over a long day. It is essential that the food a fighter eats gives him the energy to compete and that dips in blood sugar level do not leave him feeling weak or light-headed. Some simple tips to eating the right carbohydrates are:

¥ to replace some starchy carbohydrates with fibrous carbohydrates at each meal; this will increase fibre and help to fill you up
¥ to avoid large carbohydrate meals since these will make you sleepy and excessive calories will be converted into body fat
¥ always to choose wholegrain options such as brown rice or wholewheat cereal; wholegrain breads are always higher in nutrients and have a much lower glycaemic index (the rate at which sugar is released into the blood)
¥ to restrict starchy carbohydrates in the evening meal where fat loss is a goal since the need for an energy source at night is limited.

There is a common saying in sports nutrition: eat breakfast like a king, lunch like a prince and dine like a pauper, adding in two snacks for a well-balanced day. Skipping some meals and eating only one or two large ones a day results in poor energy levels, poor appetite control, muscle loss and uncontrolled blood glucose. Eating five smaller meals each day, and including protein at each, helps to control hunger levels, moods, blood glucose levels and to prevent long-term fat storage. Try to eat your last meal before 8 p.m.; to go to bed while digesting your dinner is a poor recipe for a good night s sleep and encourages the conversion of calories into body fat.

Most classes for Brazilian jiu-jitsu will be in the evening because, obviously, they are usually put on when people are not at work. This means that most students will train then and often find that they will not get back from training until late at night. What is more, they are likely to have been working hard physically and are hungry. This is where moderation is so important and yet most difficult to practice. A small meal containing plenty of protein is what is required; the protein should suppress appetite and help to fuel the recovery of bruised and damaged tissue.

Fibre

Fibre is so much more than a daily bowl of bran cereal. It is made up of indigestible plant matter that is not available as an energy source. There are two types of fibre: soluble and insoluble. Insoluble fibre has a bulking effect and found in foods such as oats, vegetables, wholewheat flour, bran and fruits with edible seeds. Soluble fibre is inclined to form a gel, retaining water in the bowel, keeping the stool soft and is found in foods such as pulses, barley, bananas, apples, citrus fruits and berries. Fibre has been identified as having many beneficial effects including the control of blood glucose, the lowering of blood cholesterol, improved bowel health and even appetite control. It has the added benefit of improving the digestion, the absorption of essential nutrients and the reduction of swings in blood-sugar levels. On average, we consume between 10 and 20g of dietary fibre a day, but ideally we should consume at least 20 to 40g. If you think that your fibre intake needs some serious attention, increase your intake gradually each day and make sure that you are well hydrated since fibre retains water in the bowel.

Fruit and Vegetables

A word of warning: do not replace all your servings of vegetables with fruit, aim for four to five servings of vegetables each day and one to two portions of fruit. The vegetables that grow above ground have a high dietary fibre content. In addition, they contain antioxidants and phytochemicals that help to reduce the risks of heart disease and many cancers. More than any other foods they contain essential vitamins and minerals, such as vitamin C and potassium for good health and disease prevention. Balance your vegetable intake between the orange/red and the green varieties. The more colourful the meal, the healthier it usually is, and, as an easy rule, the darker and brighter the colour of the vegetable, the more vitamins, minerals and fibre it will contain. For example, compare lettuce with the deep, dark green of spinach or the bright orange of carrots. Vegetables may be eaten raw, and cooking most of them conveniently takes only a few minutes if you steam, stir-fry or microwave them. Fruit and yoghurt or fruit with nuts and seeds make excellent and healthy snacks. Choose fresh, organic produce wherever possible.

For the Brazilian jiu-jitsu fighter a healthy diet is important, but there it is also the equally important issue of weight control. Rather than getting into the cycle of blood-sugar rises and falls described above, fruit and vegetable snacks are a superb way of providing the fighter with the calories he needs, but with a steady release of sugar into the blood (simple carbohydrates with high sugar contents are known as empty calories because they have no real nutritional value). Fruit and vegetables provide the energy a fighter needs, but also vitamins, minerals and an excellent source of water.

Promoting Protein

For a Brazilian jiu-jitsu fighter at least 20 to 25 per cent of his daily energy intake should come from protein. It should be included at every meal as this will help to control blood-glucose levels, support muscle tone and improve appetite control. It is vital to choose from a wide variety of protein sources. Eggs are rich in nutrients, portable, cheap and a high quality source of protein. Choose meat and poultry that is lean but avoid pork since it is the fattiest of red meats. Also avoid prepared meals and processed meat such as p tes, salami and sausages. Fish is a superb source of protein, it is low in fat, and some fish have the added advantage of being high in omega-3 fatty acids, but avoid deep-fried fish products that have been coated and battered. If fat loss is a goal, use fish tinned in mineral water rather than in oil. Grill, bake, steam or poach fish in preference to frying it. Try to avoid farmed fish but choose wild and organic fish whenever possible.

Peas and beans (legumes) are excellent sources of protein and fibre, especially when combined with whole grains, such as brown rice and lentils or houmous with wholewheat pitta bread. Most plant proteins do not contain all the essential amino acids, while animal protein does. However, combining different sources of plant protein helps to solve this problem. Plant proteins are low in fat and release sugar into the blood slowly. Baked beans release sugar slowly and are cheap, convenient and easy to store. Serve as a filling for baked potatoes or on toast.

Nuts are also a useful protein source, but they should be eaten in moderation since they also have a high essential fat content. Choose a mixture of almonds, pecans, walnuts, Brazil nuts, hazelnuts and cashews, but include too pumpkin, sunflower and sesame seeds. Add them to a salad or stir-fry or eat as a snack. Avoid nuts that have been roasted in oil or are salted.

Soya is an excellent form of protein and you should try to include it in the diet. Tofu is a bland, tasteless food that can be preserved, flavoured and cooked in a multitude of ways so that it can take on the flavour and texture of the ingredients it is combined with. Soybeans are among the foodstuffs that contain isoflavones, a group of chemicals that have a mild influence on the hormonal balance in the body. Soya milk and soya yoghurt can work well as dairy substitutes. Eating soya products may influence a number of diseases, including breast cancer, osteoporosis, heart disease and prostate cancer. Women with endometriosis are advised to limit their intake of soya.

For the Brazilian jiu-jitsu fighter the maintenance of good muscle tone and strength is vital. If a fighter tends to starve himself then he will tend to lose muscle tissue rather than body fat. In fact, in some cases where a fighter has starved himself quite severely to achieve a lower weight category his weight fell because of muscle loss but his body fat stores actually increased. The fighter may weigh less, but his power to weight ratio has obviously fallen and this can only have a significant and long-lasting, detrimental effect on his performance. Protein should be at the core of the fighter s diet because it is so important in maintaining muscle while also keeping a low body fat.

Anti-nutrients

These are substances that deprive the body of more nutrients than they provide. Smoking is a classic example, active or passive, since it has a profoundly detrimental effect. Alcohol is high in calories and leads to low blood sugar and dehydration. National guidelines suggest that women should not exceed fourteen units per week and men should not exceed twenty-one, the less alcohol you drink the healthier you are. A glass of red wine per day may have some health benefits but these can be achieved elsewhere. If it is socially difficult for you to avoid drinking on occasion, alternate your drinks with a mineral water or cut your drinks with a soda or water.

Caffeine is found in tea, coffee, chocolate and colas. It is a stimulant, increasing heart rate and blood pressure. It also irritates the stomach and can cause headaches and insomnia. To drink more than eight cups of coffee a day would be cause enough to result in a drugs test failure by the International Olympic Committee. You should choose alternatives, such as herbal or fruit teas, fruit juice and water, the best choice of all.

Our diets are high in salt. It can increase blood pressure and water retention. Prepare and cook food with the smallest amount or with no salt at all. Limit food intake in foods high in salt, such as crisps, salted nuts, bacon, and cured meats. Use garlic, lemon juice, chilli, ginger and fresh herbs as alternatives to salt for flavouring. Try a potassium salt to replace table salt.

This section of the chapter is important for anyone who wishes to be healthy and follow a healthy diet. By writing this chapter I have highlighted the importance of good nutritional practice for everyone, whether he is a martial artist or not. However, Brazilian jiu-jitsu is a physically demanding sport where, at a competitive level, control of your body weight is so important that it cannot be ignored. Any student of it should be aware of how to treat his body properly, because he will not be able to practise the art over a number of years and learn the complicated techniques that are central to it unless he keeps himself fit and healthy. It usually takes a good, talented but above all committed student a minimum of ten years to get his black belt. Brazilian jiu-jitsu is a fighting art so the student will not get his black belt by just knowing how to perform all the techniques he will have to learn. Just as in judo, the Brazilian jiu-jitsu fighter will have to prove his worth under competitive conditions on the mat; in other words, he will quite literally have to fight his way to a higher belt. If you do not pay attention to your health and conditioning, you will not make it to the next grade. Eat properly and you will enjoy your jiu-jitsu more, enjoy better health and maybe just give yourself the chance you need to get above blue belt. It is obvious that any Brazilian jiu-jitsu fighter who wishes to remain healthy and in good physical condition must take note. Good dietary habits will keep him healthy, and it is this sound basis of good health that allows a fighter to continue to practise his art for years and years.

13 Train Like a Brazilian Jiu-Jitsu Fighter

Brazilian jiu-jitsu can be a physically demanding martial art to practise, particularly if you are going to take it seriously and to compete. It is important that you pay attention to your health and your level of fitness if you are going to continue with it over a number of years and remain free from injury. However, many will take up a sport to improve their level of fitness because they find the gym boring and also find it hard to exercise regularly unless they are enjoying an activity such as football, tennis or a martial art. If you take up Brazilian jiu-jitsu as a hobby to enjoy, learn new skills and improve your fitness it will not be necessary to obtain and maintain the relatively high levels required for competition. However, it is still vital that if you want to stay injury-free, train regularly and enjoy your sport on a regular basis, that you train and exercise correctly, whatever your level of fitness and skill. Brazilian jiu-jitsu is a contact sport and it is inevitable that you are going to get some bumps and bruises along the way. You need to be sensible with your training and to know when to train and when to rest. Brazilian jiu-jitsu is a martial art that focuses on attacks to the joints of the body, if you have a tender or swollen joint, common sense should tell you that you should not train because to do so with such an injury will only make the problem worse, particularly if your injured joint is put into a lock.

The purpose of this chapter is to give you some helpful advice on how to stay fit and healthy and enjoy Brazilian jiu-jitsu, but it is only a guide to how you should approach your training, and if you are uncertain about any of the principles or training techniques discussed here you must seek the advice of your doctor, a properly qualified fitness professional or your instructor first.

The first important to point to make in any discussion of exercise and training is to differentiate clearly between health and fitness. They are not the same thing and it is important to understand why. Health defines the status of the body and how well it is functioning, in other words, is the body well or suffering from any disease or injury? Health is usually assessed by risk factors such as blood cholesterol and pressure, obesity, smoking and diet. Fitness defines the ability of the body to cope with the stress of exercise and is usually assessed by how efficiently your body operates. Fitness tests will look at how quickly you can run or what weight you can lift. It is important to understand that the exercise you do in a Brazilian jiu-jitsu class may help you to improve your fitness levels, but only a healthy lifestyle will help you to stay healthy. Brazilian jiu-jitsu has been developed over the last hundred years primarily by professional fighters. It has always therefore placed an emphasis on a healthy lifestyle and proper, sensible fitness training. This chapter is going to

Brazilian jiu-jitsu is a contact sport.

Ricardo gains a dominant position from which to control his brother.

specifically look at the training techniques that you will probably encounter in a Brazilian jiu-jitsu class and how these techniques should help improve your fitness levels and your body s ability to cope with the stress of a class. This is not a comprehensive review of all the training techniques you might employ to improve your fitness levels, but rather of the important drills and habits you should employ if you want to give yourself the best chance of staying fit, injury-free and therefore able to practise Brazilian jiu-jitsu over a relatively long period.

Any properly run class should include the following:

¥ a warm-up
¥ teaching and practice of technical skills and techniques
¥ sparring
¥ cool-down and stretching.

The duration and intensity of each of these can vary from class to class depending on the aims and goals of the instructor. For example, he may wish to concentrate more on the fighting skills of

Ricardo applies an arm bar, an elbow lock to his brother.

the students in a particular class and therefore shorten the time spent teaching specific skills so that more can be spent in sparring. So, for that particular class, the students can spend more time trying to apply the techniques that they learnt in previous classes, rather than learning new ones. In another class the instructor may wish to concentrate more on the technical skills of the students and therefore spend more time on teaching new techniques, rather than on sparring. What is important is that all four components should usually be in each class.

The Warm-up

This is an absolutely vital part of any class that involves exercise. It permits a gradual increase in the blood flow, heart rate, breathing and body temperature. A proper warm-up will help to prevent premature fatigue at high exercise intensities, which is vital if you are going to be sparring. The warm-up will allow a gradual increase in muscle temperature, which decreases the likelihood of muscle injury. If you do not warm up properly, you will increase your chance of injury. Interestingly, a proper warm-up has been shown to improve the efficiency of your neural system and therefore also of your co-ordination. Brazilian jiu-jitsu is an art that relies on good co-ordination and a high level of skill. Warm up properly and you will be able to execute your techniques more efficiently. The warm-up can also provide a screening mechanism for any potential muscle or joint problems you may have. Listen to your body if you feel tight or uncertain about a particular muscle or joint and seek proper advice because you will only make a problem worse if you continue to train with it. The aim of the warm-up is to prepare you for the class or the training session both physically and psychologically. A proper warm-up should help your body to prepare gradually for the higher level and intensity of exercise to come, and also help your mind to focus on the tasks ahead.

What is important is that any activity that you use to warm up should involve the use of the large muscle groups and is maintained for several minutes. If you are going to increase the blood flow, heart rate, breathing and temperature of the body generally it stands to reason that you must use most of the muscles in the body to warm up. So most warm-ups will include exercises such as running or skipping and will flow from one to another so that there is little rest between exercises. This ensures that the exercise stress placed upon the body is sustained. The intensity of the exercise should gradually increase as the warm-up continues so that the increases in heart rate, blood flow, breathing and body temperature are gradual. In Chapter 2 we looked at the training drills that are sometimes used in a class to warm up; you will note that most of the drills involve the use of the whole body, such as backward break falls, and this is important if you are going to increase the exercise intensity for the majority of the muscles gradually. Training drills such as the neck drill, as in Chapter 2, where only a small group of muscles are being used would not be performed at the beginning of a warm-up. This would and could not produce the relatively large bodily changes that are so important for safe, proper warm-up (the neck drill is a strengthening exercise designed to help the specific demands of Brazilian jiu-jitsu and, done properly and safely, requires the body to be already warmed up). The advantage of using the drills that involve large muscle groups is that, not only are you warming the body up but you are also practising many of the skills you will need later on in the class. A proper warm-up should last for at least 15min and you should have a light sweat at the end of it, a good indication that your whole body is warm and loose for the exercise ahead.

Teaching and Practice of Technical Skills and Techniques

The primary aim for this component is to improve your technical skills. Normally the instructor will demonstrate a technique and then you will practise it with a partner. Most complex physical movements will require a good deal of practice before you can execute them smoothly and properly. So remember, the primary aim here is to train your nervous system and not the physical condition of your muscles. The purpose of going through these techniques again and again is to teach you how to execute these movements smoothly and efficiently, with the minimum effort and strength. This is not a drill designed to increase your strength or endurance. Getting into a test of strength or speed with your partner in this part of the class will not allow you to develop the skills you need to execute the movements properly. This segment of the class comprises the time given to working on the small but important details of a specific technique. By repeatedly going over these details, such as exactly where your grip should be, you will start to learn the important skills that are so vital to being a good fighter. Remember: the pressure and speed of a fight in competition will not allow you the time or space to think about how you are going to employ a specific technique and what you should and should not be doing. Instead, these techniques need to become well-drilled habits, movements you can execute without thought, and this can only happen with proper and sensible practice over time. It is important that your partner understands this and that you work together here. Instead of trying to block or counter your move, he should give you feedback as to whether or not you are executing the move properly. If you have to use strength or aggression to execute the move or if any of the techniques you are practising feel awkward and difficult, you need to ask for help. By patiently going over the movement or the technique with your partner you are teaching your nervous system to execute the movement correctly. It is vital to your development as a fighter that you use this part of the class to work on your weaknesses and correct any technical mistakes you may be making, however small they may be. This segment is not a contest, it is where you work together to improve your individual skills. A good club will forge strong friendships between students and much of those bonds will come from working together to be the best you can. It is here that you can properly help one another to improve and develop. A club that makes you feel uncomfortable, neglected or awkward in this part of the class is not well run, and, if this is ever the case, I would recommend that you look for a different one immediately. This part of the class is not about how good you are, it is about improving your skills and technical abilities, whatever level you are at. Patient and careful practice of the techniques your instructor shows you will train your nervous system to execute these movements correctly and smoothly with the minimum of effort, which is the most fundamental principle of any jiu-jitsu training.

Sparring

This will be the most physically demanding part of the class and it is therefore essential that you are well warmed up and prepared for it. Often the slow and patient practice of specific skills earlier in the class will mean that your body may have cooled down from the warm-up. If this is the case, it is essential that you take 5 to 10min to warm up again and prepare properly for the next part of the class. Let your instructor know that you have cooled down and that you need to warm up again so that he can give you time to do so properly. If the class has students of differing technical abilities then some students may have practised techniques different from those that others have, and so some may have cooled down and others not. The instructor may not be aware of who has cooled down and who has not, so be sure to let him know that you need time to warm up again. Any good instructor will have no problem in allowing you an extra 10min to warm up again. Usually you will pair with another student and fight for about 5min; the instructor will then call time and you will move immediately to another student and again fight for 5min. This process will continue for about 40min with your moving to a new opponent every 5min.

There are two important purposes to this form of sparring: the first is that the lack of rest between fights gives the student no time in which to recover. In effect, you will spar against your fellow students for a good 40min without any significant rest. This continuous sparring is designed to make you work hard and therefore test your endurance and strength. Over time, this regular form of exercise should help to improve your fitness. The second purpose is to make you rely on your technique rather than your fitness; if you try to overpower your opponent in the first fight with strength and aggression you are soon going to be exhausted. You will have exhausted yourself in the first fight and your opponents in subsequent ones will be easily able to defeat you. Instead, you are going to have

A typical sparring session at Sleeping Storm Dojo.

to pace yourself sensibly. You will probably have about eight fights back to back in a proper sparring session and you will have to try to employ different techniques in each. As you become more and more fatigued, so your ability to dominate your opponent with strength will diminish. Fighters with good technique will be as effective at the end of 40min as they were at the beginning because they paced themselves and looked to use their technical skills to win. This is an important concept to understand and follow if you are going to enjoy Brazilian jiu-jitsu and

stay healthy and fit. We have had many students start training at Sleeping Storm Dojo who were in superb physical condition and started the sparring sessions full of energy and aggression. Yet after two fights and 10min into the sessions they were exhausted and needed to rest. They students soon learn that Brazilian jiu-jitsu is not about strength, it is about the constant flow of movement and the constant changing from one position to another, while maintaining complete control over your opponents body. This style of fighting develops good stamina

Ricardo moves swiftly from one dominant position to another so that his opponent can never settle or predict his next move.

and endurance, because the exercise is continuous and utilizes nearly all the muscles of the body.

Dominating a student of inferior skill and ability in this part of the class is of little use to you or your opponent. If you are sparring with an opponent who is not as skilled as yourself it is a wonderful opportunity for you to practise many of the techniques that you have learnt in order to get yourself out of difficult positions. You can give your opponent a dominant position, try to escape and then reverse the situation. This allows your opponent to try his skills in a dominant position against a better opponent and you the opportunity to test your skills under pressure. At Sleeping Storm, Ricardo often tells the more skilful students that they are not allowed to submit their less skilful opponents in sparring. Instead, these more skilful ones are allowed to fight only for a more dominant position and then sacrifice it to their opponents so that they have to go through the whole process repeatedly. This means that the more skilful get some useful practice and test their positional skills, while the less skilful get the opportunity to go for and develop dominant positions against better opponents. Rather than having a predictable and boring fight, where the better student just dominates and constantly submits his opponent, both fighters can practise their skills and techniques. This will make sparring much more enjoyable for everyone and reduce the likelihood of injury, because each student will be trying to use proper techniques and control rather than brute strength.

Ricardo sacrifices the dominant position to his brother so that he has an opportunity to try to pass Ricardo's guard.

Cool-down and Stretching

A proper cool-down and stretch is an essential component of any training session. After an intense session of exercise there will be a relatively high concentration of adrenalin and exercise hormones in the blood. The heart rate, breathing and body temperature will all be elevated and you need to reduce them gradually. Before you begin to stretch you need to walk slowly around the mat for at least 5min and to gradually lower your heart rate, breathing and the exercise hormones in the blood. This will reduce any immediate post-exercise tendency for muscle spasm or cramping, it will also help to prevent the pooling of the blood in the veins and arteries of your limbs and ensure adequate circulation to the heart and brain, thereby reducing the likelihood of post-exercise light headiness or fainting. It is only after you have gradually reduced your heart rate and breathing for at least 5min that you should start your stretching exercises. Take your time to recover properly and feel comfortable with your heart rate and breathing before you do anything else.

Proper stretching is vital in helping to prevent delayed muscle stiffness and your body to recover from the stress and strains

Each class will end with a proper stretching session.

Ricardo gives clear verbal and visual instructions on how to perform each stretch correctly.

It is vital that you can relax during each stretch if you are going to stretch properly.

of your training session. Stretching is designed to maintain or improve your flexibility. Flexibility is defined by the ability of each of joint to move freely through a full, normal range of movement, and the purpose of stretching is to maintain this range of movement. In most cases, the primary determinants of a joint s range of movement are the ligaments and tendons surrounding and protecting it. If these are too loose then the joint will have an excessive range of movement, they will not be able to protect the joint properly and it will be vulnerable to injury and arthritic degeneration. And if the ligaments and tendons are too tight then the joint will have a limited movement range and it will be vulnerable to arthritic degeneration, and the joint, tendons and ligaments will all be vulnerable to injury. Stretching after exercise is vitally important because after it the muscles, tendons and ligaments often adapt to a shortened position due to the repetitive contractions of the muscles

that have taken place. The primary aim of stretching is to return the muscles, tendons and ligaments to their normal resting length. The type of stretching most commonly employed to achieve this is the passive in which you hold a comfortable stretch position and then relax. It is vital that if you are going to stretch properly and safely that you can relax the muscles that you have been stretching. If you feel uncomfortable in any stretch position you will not be able to relax the muscles and this will prevent you from stretching the very muscles, tendons and ligaments that you want to stretch. Your stretching will then be a waste of time because you will not be returning the muscles, tendons and ligaments to their normal resting length. The most effective way to stretch comfortably is to use what is called a low-force, long-duration stretch. By holding a comfortable stretch for at least 40 to 60sec your muscles can relax properly and you can then stretch your tendons, ligaments

The line-up at the end of the class shows that all shapes and sizes can enjoy Brazilian jiu-jitsu.

and muscles properly. If the stretch is a high-force, short-duration stretch you are more likely to feel pain in the muscles, be unable to relax properly and unable able to stretch your muscles, tendons and ligaments properly. You may even injure and damage yourself by trying to stretch too aggressively. Stretching is not a competition, it is about helping your body to recover after exercise and giving it the best opportunity of staying free from injury.

Stretching properly after training is important, but you must do it correctly to do it effectively and safely. Each exercise is designed to stretch the muscles, tendons and ligaments of a specific joint so that it is important that you use different stretching exercises to stretch each of the muscle groups that you have employed in training. This is where the guidance of a properly qualified instructor or fitness professional is essential. Brazilian jiu-jitsu is a martial art that directly attacks the joints of the body. Your training is going to place stress upon your joints, tendons and ligaments. You must stretch properly if you are going to keep all these structures healthy and free from injury and thus a proper stretching routine is a vital part of Brazilian jiu-jitsu training.

140

Brotherly love: will Ricardo always be able to submit his baby brother? Time will tell.

There has been a tendency over the years for instructors from all the martial arts to get their students to stretch after the warm-up. This is acceptable if the stretches are comfortable and held for a relatively short period, about 10 to 20sec. However, long, relaxed stretches of 30 to 60sec are, in my view as a sport scientist, a mistake at this early stage of the class. There is no scientific evidence that stretching before exercise reduces the likelihood of injury. The most effective way of reducing this, increasing the flexibility of the muscles and preparing your body for exercise is a proper warm-up because an elevation in body core temperature of as little as 1 to 3... will significantly increase muscle elasticity and therefore the flexibility of the muscles. In fact, there is evidence to suggest that holding long, relaxed stretches before exercise could increase the likelihood of injury. By stretching the ligaments and tendons that protect a joint before exercise you may be loosening the structures that you need with which to protect the joint during training. As your opponent is looking to put many of your joints in a lock, you do not want to be loosening the tendon and ligaments that you need to protect your joints. Proper, relaxed stretching exercises should be done at the end of each training session to help the body to recover. A proper stretching routine should help you to maintain and protect the health of your entire bodily system.

Final Comments

I hope this chapter has given you some idea of what to expect in a Brazilian jiu-jitsu class and how to approach your training sensibly and properly. It is important that you learn and develop to the best of your abilities if you are going to enjoy and persist with Brazilian jiu-jitsu. It is therefore important that you try to stay free from injury and that you approach training properly and sensibly. Brazilian jiu-jitsu is, at times, a vigorous form of exercise that, performed as part of a healthy lifestyle, will help you to keep fit. The training points discussed here constitute a brief look at some of the drills and habits you should employ if you want to give yourself the best chance of staying fit and healthy and the opportunity of practising Brazilian jiu-jitsu over a relatively long period. Our most senior member at Sleeping Storm Dojo is Harry Knowles who is still a young 84-year old. He still teaches our judo and tai-chi and will spend ages on the mat with Ricardo exchanging ideas and techniques. But despite his role and being a judo player of vast experience and knowledge, Harry makes it quite clear that he does not come down to the Dojo to teach, instead he comes down to learn and share his knowledge with his fellow students. If we approach our training properly, stay fit and always look to learn from rather than dominate and just compete against our fellow students, we may all also be blessed with the opportunity to be still practising and developing our skills at the age of 84.

The founders of Brazilian jiu-jitsu UK, Rodrigo Da Silva, Ricardo Da Silva, Edward Semple and Tim Radcliffe.

Index